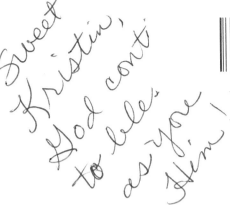

RELEASED

Finding Freedom and Peace
Through **Jesus Christ**

—EXPOSING THE ENEMY—

Paul and Carolyn Blount

Foreword by Buddy Bell

Released: Finding Freedom and Peace Through Jesus Christ
by Paul & Carolyn Blount

ISBN 978-1-4675-5507-4

$15.00
ISBN 978-1-4675-5507-4
51500>

9 781467 555074

First printing, December 2012
Cover Design by Rachel Crutchfield

ACKNOWLEDGEMENTS

We thank our dear and precious friend, Sue Henderson, for proofreading and copy editing this book. Without you, Sue, there would have been no final copy. We thank you for your love, care and support. The Lord has used you in so many ways throughout your life. Thank you for making yourself available to us.

Thank you to our mothers, Kay Watts and Evelyn Anderson for reading and commenting on this book. But, thank you most of all for your love, support and encouragement.

Thanks to Paul's brother, Kerry Blount, for initially reading the manuscript. Kerry, your notes on form and content were invaluable.

DEDICATION

We dedicate this book to our daughters, Lisa and Laura. Your love for Jesus, at an early age, led you to desire, seek, and obtain freedom long before most Believers understood the need. Lisa and Laura, you are wonderful examples of young women who have a heart for Jesus. We love you and are so blessed that God gave you to us. Thank you for your love, support and encouragement.

TABLE OF CONTENTS

FOREWORD

Too many of us Christians have this pervasive feeling that our life is not quite what it ought to be. I am not talking about what you can see on the outside, rather what you can feel on the inside. Following Jesus seems more like a burden than a blessing. In our alone and honest moments we know we are not experiencing the abundant life that our Lord Jesus promised. That is why I am so thrilled to read and recommend ***RELEASED: FINDING FREEDOM AND PEACE THROUGH JESUS CHRIST***. This is a greatly needed work from people who not only know the material; they live it. And more than just live it, they have led hundreds of others to experience freedom and peace in Christ. I am so thankful this material is now available in this form.

Paul and Carolyn Blount have been members of the church where I preach for over a decade. When God first brought them to us, I immediately could sense that they had a spirit of joy that was contagious. They were encouragers and promoters of unity and peace in the body of Christ. They had peace and they spread peace! As I got to know them I understood why. Through the challenges of life (and like all of us, they have had many) and their own restlessness they searched for and found the teaching of scripture about the path to peace. They saw our real enemy- Satan, the one who comes to "steal, kill, and destroy". Going deeper, they identified through the word of God the destructive strongholds he establishes in our lives. Most importantly, they developed Biblical and practical strategies for how to identify these strongholds and be released from them by God's power.

I want you to know that this is more than theological theory. This is more than just a well-written informative book. This is truth that can bless you. How do I know? I have witnessed it in my own life and in many other lives around me. Paul and Carolyn have been actively teaching this material in class settings and to individuals in our church body for years. I could point you to amazing testimonies. Here is the good news. You now have the opportunity to experience this for yourself! I encourage you to read this book, but do more than read- study, examine, and apply it. I am convinced it will more than live up to the promise of its title! YOU will find freedom and peace through Christ!

Because of Jesus,

BUDDY BELL
Preaching Minister
Landmark Church of Christ
Montgomery, Alabama

INTRODUCTION

If you are a Christian, this book is for you, so read on. If you are not a Christian, now is not the time for you to read it. If you want to follow Christ, pray and then talk to someone who does—a pastor, a preacher, or a good friend—and share your desire with them. They will be blessed to walk with you as you seek Him. When you know that Jesus Christ is your Savior, the Lord of your life, then come back and read the book.

Recently I was invited to deliver a guest sermon. For two weeks I wrestled with choosing a topic. It was Saturday morning and I was to speak the next day. I had thought about "Following Jesus," which is a good topic, but I didn't feel comfortable with it. It was a safe topic with multiple references and resources to help me, but I couldn't visualize an outline to start with the actual sermon preparation.

In school, I was one of those kids who processed reports, speeches, and tasks in my head. The night before it was due, I would sit down at the typewriter and it would flow out of me. Subconsciously, sometimes consciously, I had developed the theme, made the outline, gone over my points, and roughed through a couple of drafts, all in my head. When I sat down it came out finished. This carried over into adulthood, but it wasn't happening now.

My wife, Carolyn, was already up and about, but I was still in bed. I asked God, "What am I supposed to do?" and He spoke to my mind, "Your job is to expose the enemy." I got up, went to my desk, and completed the message about exposing the enemy for the next day in one sitting, straight through, with no corrections. The next day, I delivered the message and I had never felt more Spirit-led nor had I ever delivered a sermon that flowed out of me like that. Obviously, it was the work of the Lord through the Holy Spirit.

That experience confirmed some very important things to me. For about nine years, my wife and I had been teaching and ministering identity and freedom in Christ. Our initial seminar was in 2004, and from that time on, we taught large and small groups almost year round. We also prayed with and ministered individually to Christians who were being harassed by the enemy and whose lives were in turmoil.

Our ministry's focus is to bring Christians to an awareness of their identity in Christ and then help them to let Jesus set them free from the bondage of the enemy. One thing this message from God showed me was that we were on the right track and that we needed to stay on it until He told us to do something else. It also confirmed that God was very interested in this topic.

When people ask, "Why is exposing the enemy so important? Why not tell them about God, Jesus, and the Holy Spirit?" Our answer is, "We do." There is no basis for exposing the enemy if people do not understand God, Jesus, and the Holy Spirit. They must know the Truth in order to discern the lies. As Christians become more intimate in their relationship with the Father, Son, and Holy Spirit, they more readily see the deception, temptation, and accusation the enemy has been throwing their way.

The mission statement of our ministry is based on Isaiah 61:1-3. Jesus Himself read part of this Scripture in the synagogue and declared that it had been fulfilled with His coming (Lk. 4:18-21):

"The Spirit of the Lord God is upon Me, because the Lord has anointed Me to bring good news to the afflicted; He has sent Me to bind up the brokenhearted, to proclaim liberty to captives, and freedom to prisoners; to proclaim the favorable year of the Lord and the day of vengeance of our God; to comfort all who mourn, to grant those who mourn in Zion, giving them a garland instead of ashes, the oil of gladness instead of mourning, the garment of praise instead of a spirit of fainting. So they will be called oaks of righteousness, the planting of the Lord, that He may be glorified" (Is. 61:1-3).

Good news! Broken hearts can be repaired. Those who mourn can be comforted. Gladness and praise, all for the glory of the Lord! What peace and security from God, our Father, through the Lord Jesus Christ.

When I read this passage in past years, I passed by the end of the first verse, "To proclaim liberty to captives and freedom to prisoners." To me it seemed repetitive, some kind of literary device to make a point by saying the same thing two different ways. But I now believe it means so much more. If two armies, X and Y, are at war and army Y sweeps in and occupies a neutral territory, the people in that territory are called "captives." But if army Y engages army X in battle and captures one of their soldiers, that soldier is called a "prisoner." In the spiritual realm, there are two armies fighting each other—the Kingdom of God and the kingdom of darkness. But be very careful to understand that these are not two equally powerful adversaries. God and His Kingdom are infinitely more powerful than Satan and his army. However, Satan has taken the battle to this world and all those who are not in Christ are "captives." Followers of Christ, who are in the Kingdom of God, are in warfare with satanic forces. But, most of those who are in Christ have been taken "prisoner"!

Many Christians are being held prisoner by the enemy of God. They are in bondage to sin which has become so integrated in their personalities that it has developed into a stronghold. They have no joy. They have no peace. They cannot minister, encourage, or build up other Christians. They are tormented, harassed, and oppressed. They do not share the good news of the Lord Jesus with captives because they have been neutralized in the battle. The abundant life they should be living is dull at best and is miserably lacking in abundance and fulfillment. They have been incapacitated by the enemy.

The worst part is that most of them don't recognize their plight. They continue in their secret sins, going through the same routine week after week. They show up at church on Sunday, talk themselves into believing everything is okay, and compare themselves to someone who appears to be doing worse than they are. They don't understand that the enemies of God (Satan and his wicked angels) are totally satisfied, comfortable, and proud of the work they've done in rendering them impotent. The enemy gleefully supports the blind eyes and dull minds of Christians who don't even know they've been taken prisoner.

Jesus came to proclaim liberty to captives. He desires all those who exist in occupied territory to know they can be liberated! That is the "good news" of the Lord Jesus Christ. But He also came to set prisoners free. Not only did Jesus come to offer salvation, He came to overcome the enemy's work and through the Holy Spirit's power to free His people to have abundant life now! Peace, joy, and freedom from the bondage of sin and God-directed opportunities to build up, encourage, and help free other prisoners can be a daily part of the lives of those who follow Christ.

Carolyn and I were prisoners. We went to church, taught Bible classes, adhered mentally to the doctrines of our church, and generally lived our lives as pretty good people. But we were prisoners and didn't know our lives could be any different. I increasingly became more enslaved to secret sins that were frequently less secret. Carolyn was tormented by a spirit of fear. We were shackled, chained, and enslaved by the enemy … harassed, oppressed, and tormented. After 23 years of marriage, I hit the bottom of the well, and Carolyn woke up to the realization that something was terribly wrong.

Are you coming to that same realization? Is your marriage in deep trouble? Are your secret sins becoming more frequent and less secret? Is there a lack of joy and peace in your life? Are you interested in being "hot" but not holy? Are you a taker but not a giver? Do you find it more exhilarating to gossip, slander, and tear others down than to use your mouth and voice to praise God? How deep is your pit? How far do you have to go before you hit the bottom? Being enslaved by the enemy is miserable and the chains that bind you may be very heavy and getting tighter every day.

You don't have to be a prisoner, but breaking the bonds that grip and weigh you down will not be easy or casually done. It's not a chant, a mantra, or a creed to repeat. It's not magic words or heroic tasks that set us free. We have to understand who we are in Christ and what that means. We need to understand who God is and who Jesus is, and we need to understand the power of the Holy Spirit. Once we come to that understanding, we must also understand the enemy. What does he do? What power does he have? How does he imprison the people of God? These are the things we'll talk about in this book. But remember that these realizations about God, Jesus, the Holy Spirit, and the enemy will not set us free. Understanding and realization won't set us free. Jesus Christ sets us free.

And Jesus will set us free! But before He does, we need to realize that we are prisoners, understand why we are prisoners, and then come to the realization that we don't have to continue to be prisoners. We can be free. Take this journey to freedom with us. Prayerfully ask God to give you insight and protect your mind from distraction by the enemy as you read. Ask the Holy Spirit to reveal His truth, and then get ready for an abundant, joyful life. Jesus Christ will set you free!

PART 1:

WHAT DOES GOD SAY ABOUT ME?

CHAPTER ONE

IDENTITY – WHO AM I?

"Therefore, if anyone is in Christ, he is a new creation; the old has gone, the new has come" (2 Cor. 5:17).

At our seminars, toward the beginning we ask folks to take about three minutes and write a brief description of themselves. Here are examples that a couple of them have written:

"I am a husband. I am a father of two daughters. I am about 6 feet tall and about 200 lbs. I work the swing shift on an assembly line in a factory. My favorite color is blue. My favorite food is pizza. We have some animals on our land. Someday I hope to run some cattle. I am a no-nonsense kind of guy but my family thinks I'm funny. I really love my family."

"My daughter says I'm very sensitive, in a good kind of way. I try to be a kind mother and wife. I grew up here all my life. I work in our home; I don't have an outside job. My husband is gone on business trips a lot and soon my daughter will be going to college. I guess I'm not looking forward to being alone. It's kind of scary to think about. I like our church. My momma still goes to that church. My daddy left us a long time ago."

Sounds familiar, doesn't it? When asked to describe ourselves, we usually tell what we do, like the guy, or how we feel, like the woman. We all pretty much say the same things. I think it's basically because we're all in the same boat. We get up in the morning, dress, eat, brush our teeth, and we're out the door. On Saturday, we get up, eat, get dressed, do some chores, and, if you're a guy, sit back and watch a game. If you're a woman you catch up on housecleaning, laundry, and call and chat with a friend. Those who have kids may run them to ballgames. Once in a while we go somewhere else, run some errands, maybe take a little trip. On Sunday we get up, eat, get dressed, load everyone in the car, and head for church. That's the do part.

The feel part goes something like this. We wake up disturbed by a bad dream, and grumble because we don't have any clean clothes or any new clothes. We're irritated by the kids because they're not ready for school and angry at ourselves because we didn't put gas in the car so we're late for work. We sarcastically put down a coworker because they're late with an assignment, get excited because there's a new, somewhat alluring employee in our department, and rage at the other drivers on the way home. We are lonely, empty, sad, and just don't "feel" so good.

We talk about what we do and how we feel, but so often miss the most important part. That part, when understood, will truly have a great effect on doing and feeling. As Christians, we must understand who we are. Do we think all that separates us from those who are not followers of Christ is attending worship on Sunday morning and giving our lives to Jesus? Do we really understand who we are in Christ?

When a man courts a woman, he lets her know what he thinks of her. He tells her she's beautiful. He tells her she's funny. He tells her she's great to be with. Those are nice things to say, but she's probably heard them before. However, if he tells her she's a masterpiece, she's his precious treasure, and she's chosen and dearly loved, then she gets warm feelings she might never have had before, and things usually progress further in the relationship. He loves her. She loves him. She wants to believe what he says about her and will believe until proven otherwise.

Now picture this. The Creator of the Universe, the Most High God, your Heavenly Father, wraps you in His arms and tells you these things. You are His masterpiece and His precious treasure. Not only that, but He tells you He has chosen you and you are dearly loved by Him. And that's not all. He says you are righteous and holy, justified and completely forgiven, and saved and set apart. He tells you He has chosen you to be a temple where the Holy Spirit lives, blessed, adopted, and complete in Christ. By now your heart would be full and your spirit soaring, but He wouldn't be done yet.

He has so much more to tell you. This isn't fantasy or make-believe. It's reality. The great I AM is speaking this to you today and will continue with new words, in new ways, to fill you with His love for the rest of your life. When you read His Word, He tells you. When you pray and listen, He tells you. When you meet with others who are filled with His Spirit, He tells you. God continues to tell us who we are and what we mean to Him every day. To remind you of what He has to say about you, read the following list each day. Put it on your mirror. Meditate on the Word in each reference and hide these truths in your heart.

God says we are:

Adopted – **"For you have not received a spirit of slavery leading to fear again, but you have received a spirit of adoption as sons by which we cry out, 'Abba, Father!' The Spirit Himself testified with our spirit that we are children of God, and if children then heirs also, heirs of God and fellow heirs with Christ, if indeed we suffer with Him so that we also may be glorified with Him"** (Rom. 8:15-17).

Beloved – **"... knowing brethren, beloved by God, His choice of you ..."** (1 Thess. 1:4).

Blessed – **"How blessed is he whose transgression is forgiven, whose sin is covered! How blessed is the man to whom the Lord does not impute iniquity, and in whose spirit there is no deceit!"** (Ps. 32:1-2; Beatitudes -- Matt. 5:1-12).

Chosen – **"You did not choose Me but I chose you, and appointed you that you would go and bear fruit and that your fruit would remain so that whatever you asked of the Father in My name, He may give to you"** (John 15:16). I won't red the rest of the Scriptures that will be done the same.

"So, as those who have been chosen of God, holy and beloved, put on a heart of compassion ..." (Col. 3:12).

Children – **"The Spirit Himself testifies with our spirit that we**

are children of God" (Rom. 8:16).

Citizen of Heaven – **"For our citizenship is in heaven, from which also we eagerly wait for a Savior, the Lord Jesus Christ"** (Phil. 3:20).

Comforted – **"Blessed be the God and Father of our Lord Jesus Christ, the Father of mercies and God of all comfort, who comforts us in all our affliction so that we will be able to comfort those who are in any affliction with the comfort with which we ourselves are comforted by God"** (2 Cor. 1:3-4).

Complete in Jesus Christ – **"For in Christ all the fullness of Deity dwells in bodily form, and in Him (Jesus Christ) you have been made complete, and He is the head over all rule and authority …"** (Col. 2:9-10).

Delivered – **"Indeed, we have the sentence of death within ourselves so that we would not trust in ourselves, but in God Who raises the dead, Who delivered us from so great a peril of death, and will deliver us, He on Whom we have set our hope. And He will yet deliver us"** (2 Cor. 1:9-10).

Forgiven – **"Therefore let it be known to you, brethren, that through Him forgiveness of sins is proclaimed to you …"** (Acts 13:38).

Free from Condemnation – **"Therefore, there is now no condemnation for those who are in Christ Jesus"** (Rom. 8:1).

Heirs of God – "The Spirit Himself testifies with our spirit that we are children of God, and if children, heirs also, heirs of God and fellow heirs of Christ ..." (Rom. 8:16-17).

Hidden with Christ – "For you have died and your life is hidden with Christ in God" (Col. 3:3).

Holy – "Therefore, holy brethren, partakers of a heavenly calling, consider Jesus, the Apostle and High Priest of our confession ..." (Heb. 3:1).

Justified – "Therefore, having been justified by faith, we have peace with God through our Lord Jesus Christ" (Rom. 5:1).

Light of the World – "You are the light of the world. A city set on a hill cannot be hidden" (Matt. 5:14).

Masterpiece – "For we are His masterpiece created in Christ Jesus for good works, which God prepared beforehand so that we would walk in them" (Eph. 2:10).

Rescued – "For He rescued us from the domain of darkness, and transformed us to the kingdom of His beloved Son" (Col. 1:13).

Righteous – "Therefore, confess your sins to one another, and pray for one another so that you may be healed. The effective prayer of a righteous man can accomplish much" (1 Pet. 3:12).

Priests – "… and He has made us to be a kingdom, priests to His God and Father -- to Him be the glory and the dominion forever and ever. Amen" (Rev. 1:6).

Saints – "… and He who searches the hearts and knows what the mind of the Spirit is, because He intercedes for the saints according to the will of God …" (Rom. 8:27).

Salt of the Earth – "You are the salt of the earth; but if the salt has become tasteless, how can it be made salty again? It is no longer good for anything, except to be thrown out and trampled under foot by men" (Matt. 5:13).

Saved – "For by grace you have been saved through faith; and that not of yourselves, it is the gift of God …" (Eph. 2:8).

Sealed and Secure by the Holy Spirit – "In Him you also, after listening to the message of truth, the gospel of your salvation – having also believed, you were sealed in Him with the Holy Spirit of promise, who is given as a pledge of our inheritance, with a view to the redemption of God's own possession, to the praise of His glory" (Eph. 1:13-14).

Servants – "… our adequacy is from God, who also made us adequate as servants of a new covenant, not of the letter but of the spirit; for the letter kills, but the spirit gives life" (2 Cor. 3:5-6).

Sheep – "My sheep hear My voice, and I know them, and they follow Me; and I give eternal life to them, and they will never perish; and no one will snatch them out of My hand" (Jn. 10:27).

Slaves of Righteousness – **"Thanks be to God that though you were slaves of sin, you became obedient from the heart to that form of teaching to which you were committed, and having been freed from sin, you became slaves of righteousness"** (Rom. 6:17-18).

Soldier – **"No soldier in active service entangles himself in the affairs of everyday life, so that he may please the one who enlisted him as a soldier"** (2 Tim. 2:4).

Special Treasure – **"'They will be Mine on the day that I prepare My own special treasure, and I will spare them as a man spares his own son who serves him,' says the Lord of hosts"** (Mal. 3:17).

Temple of the Holy Spirit – **"Do you not know that you are a temple of God and the Holy Spirit dwells in you? Or do you not know that your body is a temple of the Holy Spirit who is in you, whom you have from God, and that you are not your own"** (1 Cor. 3:16, 6:19).

Vessels for Honor – **"Therefore, if anyone cleanses himself from these things, he will be a vessel for honor, sanctified, useful to the Master, prepared for every good work"** (2 Tim. 2:21).

Do you get the idea? When we are in Christ this is our new identity; it is who we are. We are sons and daughters of the King of the Universe. Our identity in Christ guides us in what we do and the choices we make. It affects how we feel. You may be beginning to understand your identity in Christ, but believing it is something else. The truths of God can be understood, but incorporating them into our hearts takes the power of the Holy Spirit.

There are two kinds of knowledge: imparted knowledge and revealed knowledge. Imparted knowledge is what we get from the newspaper and TV news programs. We can also receive imparted knowledge from the preacher on Sunday morning, our Bible class, or even when we read the Bible. Imparted knowledge comes through our eyes or ears and we have the facts: there are problems with the economy, a new record was set in the 100 meters, Jesse had 12 sons, and God loves me. But revealed knowledge is only accomplished through the power of the Holy Spirit. You not only know, but you believe. You not only believe, you act and incorporate it into your heart. What you say, think, and do is the evidence of the knowledge that has been revealed to you. Knowledge that has been revealed to you by the Holy Spirit is called truth.

You have probably experienced revealed truth when there was turmoil in your life or you were agonizing about a decision that needed to be made. Maybe you were caught up in sin and needed a clear conviction (not condemnation) from the Holy Spirit. So you were sitting in church, reading your Bible or praying and suddenly you were filled with the realization of what needed to be done or what God was saying about your particular situation. Many people call it a "eureka" moment, like when prospectors found a gold nugget after mining for weeks. They shouted, "Eureka!" and felt that warm, complete feeling of satisfaction. Or it's that "aha" moment when you finally see the light. That's what the Holy Spirit does for you. He reveals truth and you know God has answered your prayer or given an answer for your situation. The Bible sometimes uses the word rhema, or revealed truth.

Hiding the written Word or logos in our heart, mind, and spirit will confirm the revealed truth or rhema. They work together.

So how can truth be revealed to us through the Holy Spirit? Before God reveals His truth, He expects us to be listening, and before we can listen, we have to believe that He speaks to us. Some of the ways He speaks are through His Word, through godly Christians, and, we believe, directly into our minds and hearts. And even if we believe that God speaks to us, we must trust Him to believe that what He says is true. As we look at our identity in Christ, we will never believe that what He says about us is true unless we trust Him. Knowing God exists is a start. Knowing about God is good. But unless we trust Him, we'll never fully grasp how very special we are!

Think about it:

1. As you read through the list of who God says you are, which one touches your heart? Meditate on it. Ask God about it. Let it sink deep into your spirit.

2. Why do we believe God when He tells us He loves us, but have a hard time believing we are who He says we are? What part does the enemy play in this? Who are you going to believe?

CHAPTER TWO

TRUSTING GOD

Trusting God sounds pretty elementary, doesn't it? We say, "Of course I trust God. I gave Him my life." And we're right. If we became a Christian, a follower of Jesus Christ, then we trusted in God. We trusted that He would save us, forgive our sins, and make us holy, and He did. But there's a lot more to trusting God than salvation.

As we look at our identity in Christ, do we trust what He says? Do we believe we are holy? Do we believe we are a masterpiece, chosen and dearly loved? If we don't believe that, and so much more, we are having difficulty trusting God. We may say, "Those are good things to tell other people who are discouraged or having trouble in their lives, but I'm not sure they really apply to me." So the crux of the matter seems to be that God loves and cares for others, but not us. We may hear the lies, "What God says about His children is true for everyone else but not for me. He has chosen others, dearly loves them, and made them holy, but not me."

One reason we may not trust what God says about

who we are is that we don't feel holy. We may not feel like a masterpiece. We may not feel chosen. What we feel about what God says has very little to do with anything in the long run. We may have just turned 40 and though we don't feel 40, whatever that feels like, we still are. We may have joined the military and even though we don't feel like a soldier, we still are. Or we may have just had our first baby and though we don't feel like a parent, the fact is we are. We are children of God and He loves us, but our emotions are not reliable. Even though we may not feel special, we are.

One of the main reasons we don't trust what God says about us is because we don't know Him. If we did, we would believe every word He says, even about ourselves. If a stranger walks up to us on the street and asks us to do something out of the ordinary, we probably wouldn't do it because we don't know him. Even if we knew him, unless he had a track record of trust with us, we wouldn't do it. So when God says we are a temple for the Holy Spirit, or set apart, or righteous, the main reason not to believe Him is because we don't know Him. If we knew Him, we would know every word He speaks can be trusted. We'd know He can be trusted in everything He asks us to do. And we'd know He can be trusted forever!

Both trust and faith mean confidence, belief, assurance, security, and reliance. **"Faith is the substance of things hoped for, the evidence of things not seen"** (Heb. 11:1).

God is a covenant-keeping God. He never has and never will break His promises. His Word is trustworthy. He has a track record of keeping every spiritual agreement throughout the Bible. That is a very good reason why we can trust Him.

His Promises to us are:

> **Never failing** – Josh. 23:5-15; 1 Kings 8:56
> **Backed by God's oath** – Heb. 6:12-20
> **Fulfilled on schedule** – Acts 7:6, 17; Gal. 4: 4
> **Centered in Christ** – 2 Cor. 1:20; 2 Tim. 1:1
> **Kept by faith** – Rom. 4:20-21; Heb. 11:13-40
> **Magnificent** – 2 Pet. 1:4
> **Not slow** – 2 Pet. 3:4-13
> **The Holy Spirit** – Lk. 24:49
> **Salvation** – Acts 2:38-39
> **Heirs of the Kingdom** – Jas. 2:5
> **Life eternal** – Tit. 1:2
> **Crown of life** – Jas.1:2
> **New earth** – 2 Pet. 3:13
> **The righteous will be exalted** – Job 36:7
> **His eyes and ears are toward the righteous** – Ps. 34:15
> **He is near to the brokenhearted** – Ps. 34:18
> **The righteous will shine like the sun** – Matt. 13:43

God warns us not to trust or put confidence in weapons, wealth, leaders, people, works, or our own righteousness, but instead to place our trust in His name and His Word. Jesus Christ was sinless, perfect in obedience, trustworthy, and gave His life for us. We can put our confidence in Him.

"… not trusting in ourselves but in God, the one Who raises the dead" (2 Cor. 1:9).

"Trust in the Lord with all your heart and do not lean on your own understanding. In all your ways

acknowledge Him and He will make your paths straight" (Prov. 3:5-6).

"The Lord is good, a stronghold in the day of trouble, and He knows those who put their trust in Him" (Nah. 1:7).

"Offer the sacrifices of the righteous and trust in the Lord" (Ps. 4:5).

1. God's names: describe Him, Jesus Christ, and the Holy Spirit – the three in One. Allow your mind and spirit to meditate on these each day. He wants us to know Him intimately.

Advocate	Chief Cornerstone
All in All	Chief Shepherd
All Knowing	Comforter
All Powerful	Compassionate
All Sufficient	Commander
Almighty	Consuming Fire
Always Present	Counselor
Anointed	Creator
Avenger	Covenant Keeper
Anchor	Daddy
Author	Defender
Balm of Gilead	Deliverer
Banner	Disciplinarian
Beginning and End	Emmanuel (God with us)
Bread of Heaven	Encourager

Eternal
Faithful
Father of Mercies
Forgiving
Fountain of Living Waters
Friend
Gate
Goodness
Grace
Great High Priest
Great Physician
Healer
Head
Helper
Hiding Place
High Tower
High and lifted up
Holy
Hope
I AM
Indescribable Gift
Intercessor
Judge
Just
Keeper
Kind
King over all the earth
King of Kings, Light, Life
Lord Most High
Lord of Lords
Lamb

Light
Lion
Love
Maker
Master
Mediator
Merciful
Mighty in Battle
Maker
Morning Star
Most High
Most Holy
One and Only
Redeemer
Resurrection
Righteousness
Strong and Mighty
Strength
Patient
Peace
Potter
Power
Provider
Refuge
Rock
Salvation
Shield
Song
Support
Prince
Redeemer

Restorer Stronghold
Rescuer Sovereign
Resurrection Teacher
Rewarder Trustworthy
Ruler Truth
Salvation Understanding
Sanctifier Upholder
Sanctuary Vine
Savior Way
Sees all Wisdom
Shade Wonderful
Shelter The Word
Slow to Anger

2. God's Word is:

Inspired – "**All Scripture is inspired by God and profitable for teaching, for reproof, for correction, for training in righteousness; so that the man of God may be adequate, equipped for every good work.**" (2 Tim. 3:16-17).

Authentic (prophecy fulfilled) – "**Rejoice greatly, O daughter of Zion! Shout in triumph, O daughter of Jerusalem! Behold, your king is coming to you; He is just and endowed with salvation, humble, and mounted on a donkey, even on a colt, the foal of a donkey**" (Zech. 9:9; Matt. 21:2-5).

Without Error – "**Every word of God is tested; He is a shield to those who take refuge in Him. Do not add to His words or He will reprove you, and you will be proved a liar**" (Prov. 30:5-6).

Complete – **"You shall not add to the word which I am commanding you, nor take away from it, that you may keep the commandments of the Lord your God which I command you"** (Deut. 4:2).

Authoritative (not comparable to other books – God is the Author) – **"But know this first of all, that no prophecy of Scripture is a matter of one's own interpretation, for no prophecy was ever made by an act of human will, but men moved by the Holy Spirit spoke from God"** (2 Pet. 1:20-21).

Effective – **"For the word of God is living and active and sharper than any two-edged sword, and piercing as far as the division of soul and spirit, of both joints and marrow, and able to judge the thoughts and intentions of the heart"** (Heb. 4:12).

The evidence of faith is obedience. God always meets us on the other side of obedience. The Bible says, "Jesus learned obedience through His suffering," and we do as well. I remember times in my life when I decided to wait in obedience for God to act. Initially, I had faith that He would meet my needs and I waited, for a while. But when it seemed that God was not going to do what I thought He should, in the time I thought He should, I ended the wait and took things into my own hands. I truly did not have faith that God would come through, but when I tried to do it myself, I made a mess of it and my needs weren't met. One time, I decided to really wait obediently for God. I waited for what seemed a long time. I suffered and agonized through the wait, but continued to trust in God to meet my needs. I hurt and I cried, but I waited for the Rock of my Salvation. Just when I thought I couldn't go on, He came through! I knew that I didn't do it and He had. God came through and met my needs in a way that was right and good and perfect. He was the only one who could do it, and He received all the glory.

The next time I had an opportunity to wait in obedience, it was a little easier because I knew God would come through. My faith in Him was built and strengthened on the other side of obedience. I realized that previously I had taken control just before God brought everything together perfectly. But when I waited for Him and experienced the suffering, agony, and tears while I waited, I learned obedience. I learned that if I wait in faithful obedience God will show Himself in new and wonderful ways. As the old hymn says, "Trust and obey, for there's no other way to be happy in Jesus, but to trust and obey." Someone once said, "Life isn't about waiting for the storm to pass; it's about learning to dance in the rain."

The more we wait obediently, the more we will trust Him. At first we may be fearful, but the more we learn to trust Him the more the fear will be replaced by confident expectation and peace. Fear is a lack of faith. Over 140 times God tells us in His Word not to be afraid. The ones who should be afraid are the enemies of God. The enemy is afraid of God and he is afraid of us. If we are in Christ, live and operate in the name of Jesus Christ through the power of the Holy Spirit, the enemy has every reason to be afraid. His goal is to disconnect, disrupt, interfere, and block the intimacy and trust we have with our Father. So the enemy will do anything possible to lie and stir fear in us. He is successful only when we choose to believe the lies.

Nearly everyone we minister to has some kind of fear. Many of our fears stem from incidents in our childhood when the enemy took the opportunity to harass, torment, and oppress us. Unless these fears are dealt with and we allow Jesus to heal us, they continue throughout our lives and have an effect on everything we do. Fear is not of God. Here are some truths about why you never have to be afraid again.

"Even though I walk through the valley of the shadow of death, I will fear no evil, for You are with me; Your rod and Your staff, they comfort me" (Ps. 23:4).

"The Lord is my light and my salvation; whom shall I fear? The Lord is the defense of my life; whom shall I dread?" (Ps. 27:1).

"He will cover you with His pinions (feathers), and under His wings you may seek refuge. His faithfulness is a shield and bulwark (wall of protection). You will not be afraid of the terror by night or of the arrow that flies by day." (Ps. 91:4-5).

"He will not fear evil news; his heart is steadfast; trusting in the Lord. His heart is upheld, he will not fear, until he looks with satisfaction on his adversaries" (Ps. 112:7-8).

"The fear of man brings a snare, but he who trusts in the Lord will be exalted" (Prov. 29:25).

"Do not fear, for I am with you; do not anxiously

look about you, for I am your God. I will strengthen you, surely I will help you, surely I will uphold you with My righteous right hand" (Isa. 41:10).

"In righteousness you will be established; you will be far from oppression, for you will not fear; and from terror, for it will not come near you" (Isa. 54:14).

"Do not be afraid, little flock, for your Father has chosen gladly to give you the kingdom" (Lk. 12:32).

"For you have not received a spirit of slavery leading to fear again, but you have received a spirit of adoption as sons by which cry out, 'Abba! Father!'" (Rom. 8:15).

"The Lord is the one who goes ahead of you; He will be with you. He will not fail you or forsake you. Do not fear or be dismayed" (Deut. 31:8).

"For God has not given us a spirit of timidity, but of power and love and discipline" (2 Tim. 1:7).

"There is no fear in love; but perfect love casts out fear, because fear involves punishment, and the one who fears is not perfected in love" (1 John 4:18).

Trust in the Lord and do not be afraid. The God of All Creation is our Father. The Lord Jesus Christ, who has all authority in heaven and earth, has given us the authority to act in His name and the Holy Spirit to empower us. There is an enemy who is very angry at God and will do anything he can to get back at Him. The primary way he chooses to get back at God is to try to plague our lives through temptation, accusation, and deception. But we are not victims and his power is very limited. Read on to see why you never have to be afraid of the enemy again.

Think about it:

1. Why do you struggle with trusting God? Is it because you don't believe Him, don't know Him, or don't feel worthy?

2. Ask the Lord to help identify the fears that may be blocking you. If you give up control and trust Him, His Word, and His promises, what is the worst thing that can happen?

CHAPTER THREE

THE ORDER OF AUTHORITY IN CREATION

A s Christians, The Order of Authority in Creation is one of the most important things we need to know. The Order of Authority in Creation has a great influence on how we live our lives in Christ. It has everything to do with how we deal with temptation and harassment from the enemy. The spirit realm knows the Order of Authority in Creation, adheres to it completely, and it is the last thing the enemy wants us to know.

To understand The Order of Authority in Creation you must first walk through the order of creation from the beginning. "In the beginning God ...." We know that before anything was created, God existed. God, Jesus (the creative force, "without Him (Jesus) nothing was made that was made"), and the Holy Spirit. "The Spirit of God moved upon the waters." They existed in communion with one another. God, Jesus, and the Holy Spirit were One in authority.

We then know that God created ministering spirits

(angels/hosts) (Neh. 9:6; Ps. 148:1-5; Col. 1:16). The angels were created in an order of authority and have "free will." A contextual study of the phrase "principalities and powers" in Ephesians 3:10 indicates that it has reference to a classification of angels. Michael, Gabriel, and Lucifer were created as archangels with authority over all the hosts of angels. Michael, we are told, was the Captain of the Lord's vast army of angels (Dan. 10:12-13, 21; Rev. 12:7) and was an archangel (Jude 9). Gabriel, we find throughout the Bible, was the messenger of God (Dan. 8 and 9; Luke 1:19). Then there was Lucifer, the most beautiful angel created (Ezek. 28:11-17; Isa. 14:12-15).

After the angels were created we see that the Order of Authority in Creation was: God, Jesus, and the Holy Spirit followed by archangels and then angels.

Next, God created man and gave him authority over everything on the earth.

"Then God said, 'Let Us make man in Our own image, after Our likeness; and let him rule over the fish of the sea and over the birds of the sky and over the cattle and over all the earth and over every creeping thing that creeps on the earth'" (Gen. 1:26).

Read through Genesis 1-3 and you'll find that God verified Adam's authority by giving him naming rights. "Whatever Adam named, that was its name." Naming is a sign of authority. As a sign of our authority we have the right to name our children, our pets, our car, our land/home, and whatever else we may possess. I don't think Lucifer was very happy about this new creation, so let's go back and fill in a large gap that deals with his unhappiness.

Before man was created, Lucifer, being the most beautiful angel in heaven, was filled with pride.

"How you are fallen from heaven, O star of the morning, son of the dawn! You have been cut down to the earth. You who have weakened the nations! But you said in your heart, 'I will ascend to heaven; I will raise my throne above the stars of God. And I will sit on the mount of assembly in the recesses of the north. I will ascend above the heights of the clouds; I will make myself like the Most High.' Nevertheless, you will be thrust down to Sheol, to the recesses of the pit. Those who see you will gaze at you; they will ponder over you, saying, 'Is this the man who made the earth tremble, who shook   kingdoms. Who made the world like a wilderness and overthrew its cities, who did not allow his prisoners to go home?'" (Isa. 14:12-16).

"… You were the seal of perfection, full of wisdom and perfect in beauty. You were in Eden, the garden of God; every precious stone was your covering … on the day you were created, they were prepared. You were the anointed cherub who covers, and I placed you there. You were on the holy mountain of God; you walked in the midst of the stones of fire, you were blameless in your ways from the day you were created, until unrighteousness was found in you by the abundance of your trade. You were internally filled with violence and you sinned; therefore I have cast you as profane from the mountain of God. And I have destroyed you, O covering cherub, from the midst of the stones of fire. Your heart was lifted up because of your beauty; you corrupted your wisdom by reason of your splendor. I cast you to the ground …." (Ezek. 28:11-17). That unrighteousness was pride.

So Lucifer, now called Satan and the serpent, was cast out of heaven and a third of the host of angels who had rebelled with him were also cast out (Rev. 12:4).

"And there was war in heaven, Michael and his angels waging war with the dragon, and they were not strong enough, and there was no longer a place found for them in heaven. And the great dragon was thrown down, the serpent of old who is called the devil and Satan, who deceives the whole world; he was thrown down to the earth, and his angels were thrown down with him. And I heard a loud voice in heaven, saying, 'Now the salvation, and the power, and the kingdom of our God and the authority of His Christ have come, for the accuser of our brethren has been thrown down, who accuses them before our God day and night. And they overcame him because of the blood of the Lamb and because of the word of their testimony, and they did not love their life even to death. For this reason, rejoice, oh heavens and you who dwell in them. Woe to the earth and the sea, because the devil has come down to you, having great wrath, knowing that he has only a short time.' And when the dragon saw that he was thrown down to the earth, he persecuted the woman who gave birth to the male child…. And the dragon was enraged with the woman and went off to make war with the rest of her offspring, who keep the commandments of God and hold to the testimony of Jesus" (Rev. 12:7-12, 17).

This obviously didn't make Satan very happy. He had "great wrath" and was "enraged." Then God decided to make man and give him authority over all the earth. Where was Satan? He was on the earth, and now God had made something in His own image. As beautiful as Lucifer/Satan was, he was not made in the image of God nor given authority over all the earth. The Order of Authority in Creation had changed once more. We now have God, Jesus, and the Holy Spirit, then man, then archangels (which included Satan), and then angels.

So far, that's three changes or additions to the Order of Authority in Creation. There are two more changes which have a direct bearing on your life in Christ. You need to understand not just what changes were made in the Order of Authority in Creation, but why and how they were made.

The next change to the Order of Authority in Creation occurs in the Garden of Eden. Man has been given authority over all the earth. God has given Adam a companion, Eve, and Satan is unhappily skulking around the earth and fuming over his displacement. Then Satan tempts Eve to eat the fruit. Eve gives it to Adam who was there with her and now there's a big problem. God told them not to eat that particular fruit or they would die. Satan tells them God is lying, and that they won't die. They eat it and God is not pleased with Adam and Eve or Satan. Was He displeased because they had not obeyed Him? Absolutely! But beyond that, Adam had relinquished authority of the earth!

The apostle Paul talks about why this happened in Romans 6:16: **"Do you not know that when you present yourselves to someone as slaves for obedience, YOU ARE SLAVES OF THE ONE WHOM YOU OBEY, either in sin resulting in death, or of obedience resulting in righteousness?"** In other words, if you obey someone, you place yourself under their authority. Adam disobeyed God and obeyed Satan. When he did that, The Order of Authority in Creation changed. It was now God, Jesus, and the Holy Spirit, archangels (including Satan), angels, and then man. After chapter 3 in Genesis, this is the problem throughout the Old Testament that continued on for four thousand years. Satan had taken authority over the earth and he and his helpers would wreak havoc throughout those four thousand years. Then the most wonderful thing happened. Jesus came to rescue us!

Jesus is our Lord. He is called Savior, Redeemer, Son of God, and many more beautiful names. But there is one name we don't think about often. Jesus is also called **"the last Adam"** (1 Cor. 15:45). Adam disobeyed. Jesus obeyed. Adam sinned. Jesus was perfect. Adam had authority and gave it up. Jesus had authority, gave it up, and got it back. Jesus was born, lived a sinless life, died on the cross as a perfect sacrifice, rose from the dead, and ascended back into heaven. After His resurrection and glorification, He said; **"All authority has been given to me in Heaven and earth"** (Matt. 28:18).

Jesus became flesh/man and was under the authority of Satan on the earth. How do we know He was under the authority of Satan while on the earth? Because being a man, Jesus had to die a physical death. He rose from the dead because death/Satan could not hold him. Satan couldn't keep Him after death because Jesus had never obeyed him. **"The wages of SIN is death"** (Rom. 6:23). Because of His obedience to His Father, Jesus rose from the dead and was given authority over heaven and earth. But the final change in The Order of Authority in Creation was not the movement of Jesus. He, as in the beginning, went back to reign with His Father and the Holy Spirit. We always thank God that our sins were forgiven by the sacrifice of Jesus. We say that we are redeemed, but we were also restored!

Jesus, by His sacrifice, restored us to where God had intended us to be. **"But God being rich in mercy, because** of His great love with which He loved us, even when we were dead in our transgressions, made us alive together with Christ (for by grace you have been saved) AND RAISED US UP WITH HIM AND SEATED US WITH HIM IN THE HEAVENLY PLACES IN CHRIST JESUS, so that in the ages to come He might show the surpassing riches of His grace in kindness toward us in Christ Jesus" (Eph. 2:4-7).

Christ is in us and we are in Christ. He has redeemed and restored us. The Order of Authority in Creation is final until the return of Jesus. Here it is: God, Jesus, and the Holy Spirit, then THOSE WHO ARE IN CHRIST, then archangels, then angels, and then the worst place in the order of authority that we would ever want to be … those who are NOT in Christ.

If we are in Christ, we have authority over the entire demonic realm, not because of anything we have done, but because of what Jesus has done for us. We have authority to act in the name of Jesus Christ and through the power of the Holy Spirit. The Order of Authority in Creation is the last thing Satan and his helpers want us to know, because if we act in the name of Jesus Christ and in the power of the Holy Spirit, Satan and his helpers MUST obey us. They must stop harassing, tormenting, and oppressing us. We no longer have to be victims. Some might think, "Well, Satan was just so strong that I couldn't overcome." Jesus said, **"He that is in Me is greater than he that is in the world"** (1 Jn. 4:4). Once you realize who you are in Christ and start living and acting in the authority He has given you, your life will never be the same.

Satan has used the world system and spent a lot of time to make us fearful and to believe that he's in control. Look at all the occult and horror movies: "The Omen," "Rosemary's

Baby," "The Exorcist," "Stigmata," and "The Exorcism of Emily Rose." All these movies depict Satan as sneaky (which he is) and crafty (which he is) and so powerful (which he isn't) that we'll be unable to resist his will. This is a lie. Satan is a created being and he is under the authority of God, Jesus, and the Holy Spirit, AND he is under the authority of THOSE WHO ARE IN CHRIST. Always remember this: IT IS JESUS' AUTHORITY AND THE HOLY SPIRIT'S POWER, not ours. We have it because we are His. We have it because He has redeemed and restored us. We have it because He has gifted us. We do not act in our own power but in the power of the Holy Spirit. We do not act in our own name; we act in the name of Jesus Christ.

"Therefore also God highly exalted Him and bestowed on Him the name which is above every name, that at the name of Jesus every knee should bow, of those who are in heaven, and on earth and under the earth, and that every tongue should confess that Jesus Christ is Lord, to the glory of God the Father" (Phil. 2:9-10).

Here is a chart of the Order of Authority in Creation:

In the Beginning
GOD, JESUS, HOLY SPIRIT

Before Creation
GOD, JESUS, HOLY SPIRIT
ARCHANGELS (Michael, Gabriel, Lucifer)
ANGELS

THE ORDER OF AUTHORITY IN CREATION

After Creation
GOD, JESUS, HOLY SPIRIT
MAN
(Michael, Gabriel) ARCHANGELS (Lucifer/Satan)
Angels of the Lord   Angels of Darkness

After the Fall
GOD, JESUS, HOLY SPIRIT
(Michael, Gabriel) ARCHANGELS (Satan)
Angels of the Lord   Angels of Darkness
MAN

After the Resurrection of Jesus!
GOD, JESUS, HOLY SPIRIT
THOSE WHO ARE IN CHRIST
(Michael, Gabriel) ARCHANGELS (Satan)
Angels of the Lord   Angels of Darkness
THOSE WHO ARE NOT IN CHRIST

For the last two thousand years or so, Satan and his helpers have been operating under one big lie ... that they are more powerful than any man on the earth, even more powerful than those who are in Christ. As long as people believed their lie, they were in power because their power is in the lie. Once the lie is uncovered and exposed, power is lost. To confess is to agree with God about sin. Have you ever wondered why the Bible says in James 5:16, "Confess your sins one to another ..."? It isn't because it's a nice thing to do or because it'll make you feel better. It will, but that's not the reason.
The reason we confess our sins is because when we do, Satan can't blackmail us, threaten us with exposure, or harass us in

55

the darkness anymore. When we confess, our sin is in the light. There's nothing left with which to threaten or to blackmail us. There is no more agony through the night, because the lies have been exposed. There are so many lies connected with hidden sin, such as: "You're so bad no one will like you any more." "God can't forgive you; you've gone too far." "You can't tell anyone; it'll ruin your reputation." All of these are lies, but Satan makes them seem so threatening. He and his helpers are so good at lies that the Bible calls him "the father of lies."

Satan has lied to us for a long time, and we've believed many, if not most, of his lies. Every time we sin it's because we believe a lie: "You'll feel better if you do that." "You'll have more if you take that." "You'll know more if you see that."

These are lies we hear again and again. We'll talk more about the schemes of the enemy in a later chapter. But let's go back to The Order of Authority for a moment.

Knowing and understanding The Order of Authority in Creation is essential in our walk with Jesus. But we may ask, "If I have authority in the name of Jesus and power through the Holy Spirit, why is my life so messed up?" As we answer that, let's look at a familiar passage on dealing with the enemy, "Resist the enemy and he will flee from you." At least that's what we think it says. What it really says is this:

"Submit to God, resist the enemy and he will flee from you" (Jas. 4:7).

That's a big difference. We'll also talk about submitting to God a little later. One of the big reasons we don't submit to God or are prevented from submitting to Him is that we have a fortress built inside of us that resists instead of submitting to God. These fortresses are called "strongholds" in the Bible.

Strongholds prevent submission to God and also invite the presence of the enemy to abide with us. Let's find out how these strongholds develop.

Think about it:

1. Did you know that as a child of God when you act in the name of Jesus Christ and in the power of the Holy Spirit you have more authority than the entire satanic kingdom combined? Who doesn't want you to know this?

2. Is there any area of your life where you are not submitting to God?

PART TWO:

WHAT DOES GOD SAY ABOUT THE ENEMY?

CHAPTER FOUR

STRONGHOLDS

We know that God is three persons -- Father, Son, and Holy Spirit. He also made us with three parts: spirit, soul, and body.

"Now may the God of peace Himself sanctify you entirely and your spirit and soul and body be reserved complete, without blame at the coming of our Lord Jesus Christ" (1 Thess. 5:23).

The spirit (pneuma) is that part of our being that has consciousness of God and the potential of fellowship with Him. It is the home of faith for salvation and spiritual achievements. It is the source of love that surpasses human understanding. It is the center of the conscience toward God and others. It provides the energy for the whole being as we are fervent in spirit, and it is also the home of wisdom and understanding. Before new life in Jesus Christ, man's spirit is dead to God and he is unable to fulfill the purpose for which he was created.

The new birth that brings about salvation occurs first

in the spirit, according to John 3:6, **"That which is born of the flesh is flesh; and that which is born of the spirit is spirit."** At salvation, God's Holy Spirit comes into our spirit. In union with Him, we are able to commune with God and worship Him. **"God is a Spirit; they that worship Him must worship Him in spirit and in truth"** (Jn. 4:24).

After salvation, our spirit unites with the Holy Spirit to bring about an increased sensitivity to things that are right and wrong. Scripture defines this function by stating, **"The spirit of man is the candle of the Lord, searching all the inward parts of the belly"** (Prov. 20:27). The candle refers to an oil lamp, and in Scripture oil is a symbol of the Holy Spirit. The spirit also searches out the innermost resources of the heart, because only for the unsaved, **"The heart is deceitful above all things and desperately wicked: who can know it?"** (Jer. 17:9). When the spirit is energized by the Holy Spirit and the heart is seeking after the heart of God, there the spiritual light and power of the Holy Spirit is free to flow through our whole being.

Our soul (psyche) is made up of the mind, the will, and the emotions. God wants His Spirit to control our souls. We are strengthened in our spirits to be mighty in God's Word. If we renew our minds with the truth of God's Word, instead of the lies of the enemy, the Holy Spirit works on our mind and it is changed. Then our will follows our mind and the emotions follow last. The Holy Spirit gives Christians the ability to work from the inside (spirit) out, while those who are not in Christ work from the outside in. In that case, the body/fleshly desires affect the emotions, which then influence the mind and will. This not only affects non-Christians but is the method the enemy tries to use on Christians.

In the Psalms, there are examples of the spirit communicating with the soul. **"Why are you cast down, O my soul (mind, will, and emotions)? And why are you disquieted in me? Hope in God: for I shall yet praise Him for the help of His countenance"** (Ps. 42:5).

The spirit also cries out for God's help for the soul. **"Unto you, O Lord, do I lift up my soul. O my God, I trust in you: let me not be ashamed"** (Ps. 25:1-2).

The mind is the battlefield. We are to be transformed by renewing our mind in His truth (Rom. 12:2), taking every thought captive in obedience to Christ (2 Cor. 10:5). We are to gird our minds for action (1 Pet. 1:13) and think on things that are honorable, right, pure, lovely, of good repute, excellent, and praiseworthy (Phil. 4:8). Saturating our minds by meditating on God's Word day and night will wash out lying thoughts opposed to Scripture and reconstruct other ideas around God's principles of truth. If we meditate on Scripture as we go to sleep, as we wake up, as we go to work, and as we relax, we will be wise and successful in everything that we do (Josh. 1:8; Ps. 1:2; 63:6; Deut. 6:7).

"Sanctify them through Your truth; Your Word is truth" (Jn. 17:17).

"Now you are clean through the Word that I have spoken to you" (Jn. 15:3).

As Christians, our bodies (soma) are the temple of the Holy Spirit and members of Christ. We are to glorify God in our body (1 Cor. 6:15-20), and present our bodies as a living and holy sacrifices to God (Rom. 12:1).

"Trust in the Lord with all your heart, and lean not on your own understanding; in all your ways acknowledge Him, and He will make your paths straight. Do not be

wise in your own eyes; fear the Lord and depart from evil, it will be health to your body and refreshment to your bones" (Prov. 3:5-8).

"A tranquil heart is life to the body, but envy is rottenness to the bones" (Prov. 13:12).

"A merry heart does good, like medicine, but a broken spirit dries the bones" (Prov. 17:22).

"'You shall love the Lord your God with all your heart and with all your soul, and with all your mind. This is the great and foremost commandment. The second is like it, 'You shall love your neighbor as yourself'" (Mt. 22:37-39). When we obey this commandment in relationships with God and others, the chemicals in our bodies balance -- homeostasis.

We know that what we allow in our minds -- lies or the truth of God's Word -- will affect our spirit, mind, will, emotions, and finally our body.

As we consider the spirit, soul, and body, let's look at an area that affects all three; strongholds.

"For though we walk in the flesh, we do not war according to the flesh, for the weapons of our warfare are not of the flesh, but divinely powerful for the destruction of fortresses (strongholds). We demolish arguments and every pretense that sets itself up against the knowledge of God and we take captive every thought to make it obedient to Christ...." (2 Cor. 10:3-5).

Illegitimate strongholds are deeply ingrained, destructive patterns of thinking, feeling, and, behavior. They are a system of thinking contrary to the Word of God. Strongholds usually start with temptation to meet a legitimate need in an illegitimate way. These temptations can come from the flesh, the world, and the enemy (I Jn. 2:16).

"Let no one say when he is tempted, I am being tempted by God, for God cannot be tempted by evil and He Himself does not tempt anyone. But each one is tempted when he is carried away and enticed by his own lust. Then when lust has conceived, it gives birth to sin; and when sin is accomplished, it brings forth death" (Jas. 1:13-15).

The Flesh – *The flesh defined is the appetites of the body. It is very clear that we have desires of the flesh. We get hungry and we eat. If we eat too much for too long and our choice of pleasure is overeating, then we are trying to meet a legitimate need in an illegitimate way. That is called gluttony, and gluttony is a sin. We have sexual desires. God has given us the structure for meeting our sexual needs, which is marriage. But if we meet these needs whenever and however we want outside of marriage, that's called fornication, and fornication is a sin.*

The World – *The world system also presents many temptations. Movies, television, magazines, and billboards are some of the obvious avenues. The internet and cell phones with texting and twitter can also be used to tempt us. The way people dress, talk, and act can be used to lead us into sin. There are many parts of the world system that expose us to temptation.*

The Enemy – *The enemy consists of Satan and his helpers. We'll talk more later in the book about him personally and his helpers (what they are, where they come from, and what they do.*

When sins become ingrained bad habits in the personality, they are called strongholds. A stronghold becomes the center of operations for the enemy in our minds and bodies. For example, consider a man who has a stronghold of lust, specifically pornography. He has viewed pornography for so long it is a habit and has become a stronghold in his mind. He seeks comfort and pleasure from it so he makes plans to get it and view it. All the enemy has to do at this point is bring pornography to his mind because it has a strong hold on him. Actually, it's the enemy who has the strong hold, and because this is his center of operations, other sins and strongholds branch off from it. The man begins to lie in order to conceal his habit from his family. He begins to watch it on the job or take time off from work to watch it. If he can't afford the pornography, he begins to steal it or steal to get it. The enemy uses the stronghold of pornography as the base of operations and easily leads the man into other sins and bondage. With so many opportunities to tempt us, the enemy utilizes all of them to his maximum advantage. But, again, all of these temptations are based on a lie. Once we buy into a lie, we've started on the road to a stronghold. Let me be very clear: we can buy into a lie for a number of different reasons.

The first is that we are deceived. The lie sounds so good that we assume it to be true. "God just wants me to be happy" turns out to be one of the most insidious lies of all. God never said he wanted us to be happy. He wants us to be content with what we have and at peace in Him. He wants us to be faithful, obedient, and filled with the Holy Spirit, but He never said He wanted us to be happy. Many people have used that lie to justify their affairs and ultimately their divorces because they bought into a lie that sounds good, but has its root in the schemes of the enemy.

We can also buy into a lie because we just want to sin.

Yes, there are times we sin because we desire pleasure. Not all the time, but there are those times when we simply decide to sin. That is called willful disobedience which is rebellion against God. And rebellion against God is **"as the sin of witchcraft"** (1 Sam. 15:23). That is very serious.

There are other lies we buy into because we don't know the truth. Instead of studying the Word of God and finding the truth about a specific subject, we listen to friends, family, or even well-meaning Christian brothers and sisters who spout words that sounds good but are as far from the truth as we can get. Like the "God just wants me to be happy" lie, these lies sound good but take us in the opposite direction from what God intended. How about, "It's okay to party and have sex as long as you have a good heart"? I think the most popular lie of all time is, "If it feels good, do it." How about when I feel bad about myself or how I look and buy into the lie that I'll feel or look better if I put someone else down? So the first time I see someone who is uglier or shorter or slower than I am, I put them down. Then I repeatedly put others down and find I have become a critical person. That is a stronghold.

Here is a list of some strongholds. Are there any on the list that may have taken up residence in your life?

Anger, fear of all kinds, anxiety, insecurity, laziness, gossip, alcoholism, sexual bondage, depression, bitterness, pride, rebellion, deception, obsessive thought, compulsive action, eating disorders, and bad habits.

God wants to be our stronghold. As our only legitimate stronghold, He is a hiding place, a place of fortification, shelter, and protection. He is the only legitimate stronghold. Any thing or person used as a stronghold is an idol.

"The Lord is good, a stronghold in the day of trouble;

and He knows those who trust in Him" (Nah. 1:7).

The enemy holds us in bondage through the strongholds that have been built and fortified with our participation in the lie. Many people don't understand the enemy and how he works. It's time we expose him!

Think about it:

1. What are the false strongholds/idols in my life?

2. Who wants to be my stronghold?

CHAPTER FIVE

THE ENEMY

Satan, Lucifer, the Devil, Prince of Darkness, Prince of the Power of the Air, and the Accuser are some of the names for the leader of the kingdom of darkness. Furthermore, when there is a kingdom, there must be followers or helpers. The Bible calls these wicked angels, demons or evil spirits. For hundreds of years some of the western world has ignored or dismissed them, but they are real. As Christians, we have no need to fear them. But we do need to know about them, understand them, and expose them.

Satan was an archangel and the most beautiful angel. The Word of God gives a very clear picture of the story of Lucifer, who desired to lift himself up to be equal and even above God. He was an archangel who apparently influenced a third of the angels to rebel with him, and they were all thrown out of heaven.

"Then another sign appeared in heaven: and behold, a great red dragon having seven heads and ten horns, and on his heads were seven diadems. And his tail swept away

a third of the stars of heaven and threw them to the earth. And the dragon stood before the woman who was about to give birth, so that when she gave birth he might devour her child" (Rev. 12:3-4).

How many angels were created in the first place? God didn't say in His Word, but if the God of all creation decided He wanted to have ministering spirits (angels) when He spoke, I believe there were millions and millions of them. Revelation speaks of **"ten thousands times ten thousands and thousands of thousands"** (Rev. 5:11). That's quite a few. A thousand thousands are a million. Ten thousand times ten thousand are a lot more than that. Always remember, Satan and his angels are created beings. They were created by God with a will to choose good or evil.

We must be familiar with the attributes of God in order to understand the enemy.

God is omnipotent, which means He is all powerful. He can do anything. Nothing and no one is more powerful than God.

"I AM the Almighty God; walk before Me and be perfect" (Gen. 17:1).

"In the Lord JEHOVAH is everlasting strength" (Isa. 26:4).

"The Lord God Omnipotent reigns" (Rev. 19:6).

God is omnipresent. That means He is everywhere. He can be everywhere at once and can see anything at any time. We cannot hide from him.

"'Am I a God who is near,' declares the Lord, 'and not a God far off? Can a man hide himself in hiding places so I do not see him?' declared the Lord. 'Do I not fill the heavens and the earth?' declares the Lord" (Jer. 23:23-24).

"Where can I go from Your Spirit: or where can I flee from Your presence? If I ascend to heaven, You are there; If I make my bed in hell, behold, You are there. If I take the wings of the dawn, If I dwell in the remotest part of the sea, even there Your hand will lead me, and Your right hand will lay hold of me" (Ps. 139:7-10).

God is omniscient. That means He is all knowing. He knows everything. He knows the hearts of all creation. He knows what was, what is, and what will be.

"... then hear from heaven Your dwelling place and forgive, and render to each according to all his ways, whose heart You know for You alone know the hearts of the sons of men" (2 Chron. 6:30).

"O Lord, You have searched me and known me. You know when I sit down and when I rise up; You understand my thoughts from afar. You scrutinize my path and my lying down, and are intimately acquainted with all my ways. Even before there is a word on my tongue, behold, O Lord, You know it all" (Ps. 139:1-4).

"Search me, O God, and know my heart; try me and know my anxious thoughts; and see if there be any hurtful way in me, and lead me in the everlasting way" (Ps. 139:23-24).

"And Jesus knowing their thoughts said, 'Why are you thinking evil in your hearts?'" (Matt. 9:4).

"... resulting in a true knowledge of God's mystery, that is, Christ Himself, in whom are hidden all the treasures of wisdom and knowledge" (Col. 2:2-3).

"... in whatever our heart condemns us; for God is greater than our heart and knows all things" (1 Jn. 3:20).

Our God has many, many more attributes. He is the

Most High. He is all loving, all merciful, and immutable (unchangeable). And remember that Jesus and the Holy Spirit are One with Him. We must know who God is in order to understand who Satan and his wicked angels are and what they can and cannot do.

Now it's time to expose the enemy. Satan is not God. Satan is not omnipotent. He is not all powerful. He can't do anything with everything. The power of Satan and his helpers is in the lie; he is the father of lies. If we believe his lies, he has power. If we don't believe them, he has no power.

Satan is not omnipresent, so he can't be everywhere. It is likely that as bad as your encounter with the enemy may have been, it wasn't with Satan himself. He cannot be everywhere. Remember the words of the apostle Peter, **"Be of sober spirit, be on the alert. Your adversary, the devil, prowls around like a roaring lion seeking whom he may devour"** (1 Pet. 5:8).

If Satan has to roam around, he is not everywhere at the same time. He is a created being and has limitations like all created, spiritual beings.

Satan is not omniscient. He does not know everything. He does not know what is in your heart. Only God knows the hearts of men. Most importantly, Satan doesn't know what you are thinking. Neither he nor his wicked angels can read your mind. They are created beings that desired the attributes of God but were never given them. Satan and his wicked angels are not omnipotent, omniscient, or omnipresent.

"Our struggle is not against flesh and blood, but against the rulers, against the authorities, against the powers of the dark world and against the spiritual forces of evil in the heavenly realms" (Eph. 6:12).

In a very broad sense, there are three basic worldviews with regard to the spirit world. Many cultures of the world fall into the first category referred to as Animism. Animism holds that spirits are pervasive in everything: trees, rocks, houses, people, gardens, mountains, rivers ... everything is controlled and affected by spirits. In these cultures the spirits are greatly feared and must be placated. Witch doctors, shamans, or medicine men usually are the mediums or go-betweens for the people. Gifts are offered and sacrifices are made to compel the spirit to deal in a favorable manner.

The second broad grouping is the Western worldview. This view holds that spirits do not exist. Any interaction with the spirit world is impossible since there is no spirit world. The enlightenment had a great deal to do with this mindset. This point of view broadly led to secular humanism which purports that man is the center of everything. Within this worldview are, oddly, some Christian groups that deny any existence or involvement with the spiritual realm. They believe in God and His Son, Jesus Christ, but the role of the Holy Spirit is very limited in their belief system. Any involvement with good or evil angels would be totally out of the question.

The third group we will call the Biblical worldview. In this worldview the Holy Spirit is active and indwelling every believer. There is interaction between angels of God and wicked angels, and between angels and people. Satan is alive and leading the army of darkness. As has been pointed out, God, Jesus, the Holy Spirit, and those who are in Christ have infinitely more power than the entire satanic kingdom combined.

Many people fall into the error of looking at the world from a dualistic point of view. Dualism says that there are two equal adversaries: good and evil. They say God is powerful on one side and Satan is powerful on the other side. Their view is that God and Satan are in conflict all the time and sometimes one wins and sometimes the other wins. Dualism is a lie from the enemy. God is God. Satan is a being created by God. God is victorious. Jesus has risen from the dead, saved us, restored us, ascended into heaven, and is seated on the right hand of God! Jesus Christ has all authority in heaven and on earth. Satan is skulking around trying to get the children of God to believe his lies. And when we do, we begin the process of becoming prisoners.

Satan has many schemes and plans to tempt, accuse, and deceive the children of God. But, ultimately, we are not his primary target. Satan tempts, harasses, torments, and oppresses us and then accuses us to God because he knows his time is short and he is very angry at God for displacing him. See Genesis 3, Job 1, and Revelation 12. Satan's ultimate desire is to get back at God. He wants to hurt God, so he makes Him sad by hurting His children.

Satan and his angels cannot read our minds. They can put thoughts in our minds, but they cannot read them.

"… and during supper, the devil having already put into the heart of Judas Iscariot the son of Simon, to betray Him …" (Jn. 13:2).

"But Peter said, 'Ananias, why has Satan filled your heart to lie to the Holy Spirit, and to keep back some of the price of the land?'" (Acts 5:3).

"Then Satan stood up against Israel and moved David to number Israel" (1 Chron. 21:1).

Spiritual communication with physical beings (us) is through the mind, but God, Jesus, and the Holy Spirit are the only spiritual beings that know what we're thinking. Satan or a wicked angels can tell us to "steal the candy" IN OUR MIND, but they don't know the temptation has been effective until we do it. They can't see the struggle in our minds as we deal with stealing the candy. They may see the expression on our face or read our body language and realize there's a struggle going on, but they cannot read our minds. Satan and his helpers have no idea that their temptation is successful until we act on it. Then they know, and if they were successful, they will ask us to do it again another time because they have found a weakness. We call this weakness an open door. They have found a way into our lives and will do everything they can to start building the stronghold.

This next point is very important. Do not try to confront the enemy in your mind. They can't read your mind, so they can't hear you. You may think, "Get away from me, Satan," but they can't hear you. Is this hard for you to believe? Let's take a look at the most intense confrontation with Satan ever recorded. The Holy Spirit led Jesus into the wilderness and Satan came to tempt Him.

"'If you are the Son of God command that these stones become bread,' and Jesus said, 'Man does not live by bread alone but by every word that proceeds from the mouth of God.' Satan said, 'If you are the Son of God throw yourself down, for it is written, "He will command His angels concerning You; and in their hands they will bear You up, so that you will not strike your foot against a stone."' Jesus said to him, 'On the other hand, it is written, "you shall not put the Lord your God to the test."' And Satan said to Him, 'All these things I will give You, if You fall down and worship me.' Then Jesus said to him, 'Go,

Satan! For it is written, "You shall worship the Lord your God, and serve Him only"" (Matt. 4:1-11).

Jesus spoke aloud. The word of God doesn't say Jesus thought. It says "Jesus said" because Jesus was speaking from a fleshly body and Satan could not hear His thoughts. Satan cannot hear your thoughts, but he doesn't want you to know it. One of his big lies is that he can read your mind and he has the upper hand. The lie is, "I can't get away from Satan because he can read my thoughts." "The Devil made me do it" is not true because he can't make us do anything. Satan has led us to believe through the help of Hollywood, books, and television shows that he knows our inner heart and we must succumb to his overwhelming power. IT IS NOT TRUE!!!

Remembering the Order of Authority in Creation, those who are in Christ have authority over Satan and his evil spirits. We must confront Satan or an evil spirit aloud, "In the name of Jesus Christ and by the power of the Holy Spirit." When we do this, they must leave us if we are in submission to God. If we are prisoners, in bondage to sin, and have given access to the enemy, Satan or his angels will not leave us alone because we have given them the legal right to torment, oppress, and harass us.

Think about it:

1. Where did Satan come from?

2. Is Satan omnipresent, omnipotent, or omniscient?

3. Can the enemy read your mind?

CHAPTER SIX

HOW THE ENEMY WORKS

There are two ways the enemy seeks access into our lives; they either trespass/break in or they are given permission or an invitation.

Let's say you are the President of the United States and you live in the White House. There are only two ways someone can get into the White House grounds. One is to trespass. A person drives his car into the fence of the White House grounds, jumps out of the car and runs toward the White House; that is trespassing. He has no legal right to be there, so the guards run him down and throw him out. In the same way, many times the enemy "intrudes" or inserts himself into our lives, i.e. he breaks in. When we are suddenly stricken with fear or anxiety about something, we can recognize that it is the enemy trying to make us fearful and anxious. Then we can immediately take action to throw him out by the authority of the Lord Jesus Christ and through the power of the Holy Spirit. The Holy Spirit is the guard at our gate and Jesus is the authority to send the enemy away. He has no right to be there, trying to force his way in.

But let's say that you, as the President, send someone an invitation to the White House. They show up, present their invitation, and are given permission to enter. They have legal permission to be there. In the same way, we, as Christians, are, at times, harassed by the enemy because we have given him permission to enter our "house."

When we leave the door to our house open, we give insects, animals, and even strangers an opportunity to come in. In the same way, if we give the enemy an invitation or permission to come into our lives, he will accept the invitation, come in, and harass us. There are at least six ways that we invite him into our lives to harass, oppress, torment, and deceive us. These can be thought of as opportunities, invitations, or permission for him to come in. Sending an invitation gives the enemy the "right" to stay with us. I'm convinced that he will stay until all these areas are taken back and he is told to leave by the authority of Jesus Christ. I believe evil spirits stay in family lines for decades until they are weakened and told to leave. Do I think Christians can be possessed by the enemy? No. An emphatic NO! Children of God, followers of Christ, are "sealed by the Holy Spirit." We are God's own possession.

"In Him, you also, after listening to the message of truth, the gospel of your salvation–having also believed, you were sealed in Him with the Holy Spirit of promise, Who is given as a pledge of our inheritance, with a view to the redemption of God's own possession, to the praise of His glory" (Eph. 1:13-14).

Satan and his wicked angels cannot own or possess us, but they will take all the territory we give them. They will gladly accept any and every invitation we offer them, happily go about the building of strongholds in our individual lives, and reside there. But, they do not possess us. They can influence, harass, torment, and discourage us when we believe their lies, but the only power the enemy has over us is when we believe the lies. The lies have to be discovered and replaced with the truth of God's Word.

There are at least six ways that we give the enemy an opportunity and legal access to wreak havoc on our lives. They are: willful disobedience, unforgiveness, emotional trauma, inherited iniquities, inner vows and judgments, and careless invasion of enemy territory.

WILLFUL DISOBEDIENCE

Willful disobedience is when we make the choice to sin even though we know it's wrong. We decide to disobey God even when we know we're doing something that He wouldn't want us to do. Willful disobedience is an invitation for the enemy to take up residence in our lives. He will use our sin as an opportunity to accuse, condemn, and blackmail us. Remember, when we willfully sin we are disobeying God and obeying the enemy. We place ourselves under the authority of the one we obey. We've all willfully disobeyed in our lives. Willful disobedience is disobedience to God and obedience to Satan and the kingdom of darkness. As we've seen, Romans 6:16 tells us that we come under the authority of whoever we obey. So when we know something is wrong and decide to sin anyway, we provide an opportunity for the enemy to come into our lives and harass us. Taking back our territory by repentance of that sin, resolving not to engage in it in the future by the power of the Holy Spirit, and asking God for forgiveness is what must happen. The enemy is weakened through these steps and has no legal right to stay. What we've done is essentially withdrawn the invitation for him to stay at our house or trespass.

"Do you not know that when you present yourselves to someone as slaves for obedience, you are slaves of the one whom you obey, either of sin resulting in death, or of obedience resulting in righteousness?" (Rom. 6:16).

UNFORGIVENESS

Unforgiveness is the biggest bait and trap of the enemy. When we harbor unforgiveness in our hearts, we are holding onto bitterness and resentment that can destroy our lives. The enemy uses unforgiveness to distort, confuse, and preoccupy our minds. Because forgiveness is the basis of Christianity, unforgiveness is the secret weapon of Satan and his helpers. Unforgiveness can give the enemy access into our lives for a lifetime through the bitterness and hate that accompanies it (2 Cor. 2:10-11). Our hearts can become hardened, which gives the enemy a stronghold (Eph. 4:26-27; Matt. 18:34). Unforgiveness can spiral downhill into bitterness which leads to outbursts of anger, then rage, then making a public scene, then slander, and finally hatred (Eph. 4:31). This root of bitterness will also bring ungratefulness, a critical attitude, revenge, mistrust, depression, and selfishness. Unforgiveness has been compared to drinking poison and hoping it hurts the person toward whom we harbor bitterness. It damages our relationship with God (Matt. 6:9-15; Ps. 103:1-2). Forgiveness is a choice of our will and can be done only with the help of the Holy Spirit (Rom. 12:17-21; Mk. 11:25).

We have been commanded to **"Be kind, compassionate to one another, forgiving each other, just as Christ forgave you"** (Eph. 4:32). God will not forgive our sins if we do not forgive others; but if we forgive others, He will forgive us (Matt. 6:14-15). We must forgive others because God in His great mercy and compassion has already forgiven us.

EMOTIONAL TRAUMA

Emotional trauma can be inflicted on us through abuse, neglect, or accident, and usually happens through no fault of our own. Emotional trauma evokes pain when we remember the event. The enemy encourages us through these traumas to doubt God ("Why did He let this happen to me?"), to doubt others ("How can I ever trust anyone again?"), or to blame ourselves ("I must have done something that made them do that to me.")

INHERITED TENDENCIES/ INIQUITIES

Inherited tendencies or iniquities are the tendencies, propensities, and strongholds, which are passed down through the generations in our own family. For example, if my great grandfather was an alcoholic, my grandfather was an alcoholic, and my father was an alcoholic, then I will have an inherited iniquity giving me a tendency or propensity toward alcoholism. This is more than just a possibility. Examples of inherited iniquities are anger, sexual bondage, fear (of any kind), abuse, and many more. The enemy encourages us to continue the sins of our forefathers. When we do, the particular enemy that harassed our family for generations will stay with us and expect to continue with our children. The good news is that through prayer, these can be ended in us and our children!

INNER VOWS AND JUDGMENTS

There are two kinds of inner vows. They can be godly or ungodly. Godly vows are from the leading of the Holy Spirit when we vow to surrender our life to Jesus Christ and when we say our wedding vows.

Most vows are ungodly. An ungodly vow is a determination made by our soul (mind, will, and emotions) that declares control around an area of our life by our own effort. It leaves out God's will and the fact that only He is in control. It is a strong inner declaration of protection based on fear to avoid pain for ourselves. It stems from a stubborn or prideful heart and can be done in our minds or spoken aloud. Many people do this without realizing it, especially with relationship to trauma or unforgiveness.

Some examples are: "I will never be poor again!" … "I will never let a man hurt me like my daddy hurt my mother." … "I will never treat my children like my parents treated me," … "I am not going to stay in a marriage where I am unhappy." … "I will stay out of debt if it's the last thing I do." … "I give up trying to control my weight because I will always be overweight." … "I will never be like him." … "I will never marry a woman like my mother." … "I will never trust a man again in my life."

Inner vows usually carry a judgment of some kind: "Dad is cruel" or "my teacher is mean" or "women are bad."

Even if it is a vow to do a good thing, an inner vow is putting us in control and excluding trusting in and relying on God. Oftentimes the words "never" and "always" are used.

"Therefore you have no excuse, everyone of you who passes judgment, for in that which you judge another, you condemn yourself; for you who judge practice the same things (Rom. 2:1).

It is healthy to not want to be like someone who is abusive. However, it is passing judgment on a person to make a vow about them. It is healthy to say, for example, "God, in your grace and mercy, help me not to abuse others like I was abused."

CARELESS INVASION OF ENEMY TERRITORY

Careless invasion of enemy territory is "hanging out" with the enemy. Bars, strip clubs, casinos, and drug houses are examples of enemy territory. There are people who go to bars with no intention of getting drunk because drunkenness is the sin. But many of them have done so because of the influence of the enemy. The only purpose for going to a strip club is lust. The enemy will attach themselves to us and encourage the pursuit of lust during the visit and even after leaving the club. Casinos are enemy territory because he will encourage those who go there to wager more than they should. Many compulsive gamblers, those who are addicted to gambling, have lost their homes, jobs, and/or families because of the influence of the enemy in a casino. Areas for drug dealing, sections of town, and specific houses or buildings are for the purpose of obtaining illegal drugs and using them to experience an altered state of consciousness. The enemy will always take advantage of anyone who gives up control of their consciousness to come in and torment them.

As Christians, upon entering any of these places carelessly (hanging out, just for fun, trying it out) we will immediately feel a change in atmosphere, an attachment. That attachment is the enemy connected to that particular location joining us and trying to encourage sinful behavior. It's similar to flies that are drawn to rottenness.

Now that we are aware of the openings we give the enemy, let's look at one more aspect of our lives that gives him an opportunity to accompany and use us; the words we speak. God's words are so powerful that He spoke all of life into existence in Genesis 1 and 2. **"God speaks life to the dead and calls things that do not exist as if they already did"** (Rom. 4:17).

"For as the rain and the snow come down from heaven, and do not return there without watering the earth and making it bear and sprout, and furnishing seed to the sower and bread to the eater; so will My Word be which goes forth from My mouth; it will not return to Me empty, without accomplishing what I desire, and without succeeding in the matter for which I sent it" (Isa. 55:10-11).

His Word is similar to rain that produces fruit. Just as water strengthens a flowering plant, God's Word produces life in the hearts of sinners.

"I will bow down toward Your holy temple and give thanks to Your name for Your loving-kindness and Your truth; for You have magnified Your Word above all Your name" (Ps. 138:2).

"Obey Me and live. Guard My Word as your most precious possession" (Prov. 7:21).

"… for you have been born again not of seed which is perishable but imperishable, that is, through the living and abiding word of God" (1 Pet. 1:23).

Just as God's words have power, so do the words we speak. Death and life are in the power of the tongue. The words that we speak hold life or death for us and for those to whom we speak.

In 1 Samuel 17:45-47, David spoke aloud for Goliath and all to hear the truth that the Lord would deliver Goliath into David's hands to die, so that all the earth would know there is a God in Israel, and that the battle belongs to the Lord.

When He was being tempted in the desert, Jesus spoke aloud the truth of God's Word in Matthew 4:1-11. When He told Satan three times, "It is written …," Satan gave up and left Him. When we speak God's Word as believers, we are in agreement with Him. We can be on the offense and move forward against the enemies of God by speaking aloud the truth of God's Word. Each time a negative, discouraging thought comes to your mind that does not agree with God's Word, speak the truth of His Word aloud. The enemy will give up for a time and the thought will leave. For example, when the enemy attempts to make us afraid, we can speak aloud the truth, **"God has not given me a spirit of fear, but of power and love and discipline"** (2 Tim. 1:7).

In Proverbs 18:21, we are told that **"Death and life are in the power of the tongue, and those who love it will eat its fruit"** (Prov. 18:21). Many people have no concept of the weight of their words. You may remember unkind words said to or about you and how they hurt. Many times these words are said without thinking or in anger. Sometimes they are said out of hurt, sadness, or revenge. You may also remember speaking words like this toward someone else. Threats can be spoken in fear to create fear and control the other person or circumstance. Words spoken with sarcasm or cowardice in the disguise of "it's only a joke" can be brutal to another person and cause scarring (Prov. 23:18-19) – **"Like a madman who throws firebrands, arrows and death, so is the man who deceives his neighbor, and says, 'was I not joking?'"**

Words can be thoughtful or impulsive and have the power to heal or wound … be positive or negative … encourage or discourage … bring peace or fear … lift up or tear down … be a soothing balm or poison … bring life or death … build faith or unbelief … bring praise or destruction … be from the Holy Spirit or from the enemy … be light or darkness … be truthful or lies … bring blessing or condemnation … be trustworthy or break confidences … show mercy and forgiveness or expose bitterness … be wise or foolish … bless or curse … judge or sustain … be gentle or harsh … delight or criticize … create or destroy.

"I will guard my ways that I may not sin with my tongue; I will guard my mouth as with a muzzle …" (Ps. 39:1).

"Set a guard, O Lord, over my mouth; keep watch over the door of my lips" (Ps. 141:3).

"A gentle answer turns away wrath, but a harsh word stirs up anger" (Prov. 15:1).

"A man has joy in an apt answer, and how delightful is a timely word!" (Prov. 15:23).

"Whoever guards his mouth and tongue keeps his soul from troubles" (Prov. 21:23).

"He who goes about as a slanderer reveals secrets, therefore do not associate with a gossip" (Prov. 20:19).

"Like apples of gold in settings of silver is a word

spoken in right circumstances" (Prov. 25:11.)

"The Lord God has given me the tongue of disciples, that I may know how to sustain the weary one with a word" (Isa. 50:4).

"And I say to you, that every careless word that men shall speak, they shall render account for it in the day of judgment. For by your words you shall be justified, and by your words you shall be condemned" (Matt. 12:36-37).

"It is the Spirit who gives life; the flesh profits nothing; the words that I have spoken to you are spirit and are life" (Jn. 6:63).

"If anyone thinks himself to be religious and yet does not bridle his tongue but deceives his own heart, this man's religion is worthless" (Jas. 1:26).

"Like a bit in a horse's mouth, or the rudder of a ship, or a forest fire from a small flame, so is the body controlled by the tongue" (v.8-9). "No one can tame the tongue; it is a restless evil and full of deadly poison. With it we bless our Lord and Father; and with it we curse men who have been made in His image" (James 3:4-9).

"... But let everyone be quick to listen, slow to speak and slow to anger; ..." (Jas. 1:19).

Words are powerful and carry great weight and meaning. We all must watch our words and speak life to ourselves and others.

Think about it:

1. What are the two ways the enemy has access into our lives?

2. What are the "open doors?" Ask the Lord to show you which of the "doors" are open to give the enemy an opportunity.

3. When you speak, are your words critical, harsh, angry, condemning, hurtful, negative, tearing down, sarcastic, prideful, death, careless, thoughtless, revengeful, bitter, and full of slander or gossip?

4. Ask God to help you each day to speak only life, blessings, and peace to yourself and all others. Ask Him to guard your tongue.

PART THREE

WHAT DOES GOD SAY ABOUT MY HEART?

CHAPTER SEVEN

PRIDE

Pride is the root cause for many sins. It was the original sin. It was the reason Lucifer was cast down out of heaven because he tried to make himself equal to God. Pride keeps self on the throne. It enslaves us in the sin that Christ came to free us from. It blinds and deceives us. Pride seeks the approval of people instead of God. It is doing what I want to do when and how and where I want to do it. There are two forms of pride. One is easier to detect as it is haughty and is more visible and outward, similar to a strutting rooster. It is a focus on self that is expressed in thoughts, words, and actions. It focuses on our knowledge, strength, and possessions. The other kind of pride is an inward attitude, which is a focus on our inner pain and feelings of rejection that develop into self-pity resulting in an inability to see anything except our own needs and feelings. Therefore, we cannot reach out to others.

Pride causes difficulties in our relationships with God and others.

"By pride comes nothing but strife, but wisdom is with those who receive counsel" (Prov. 13:10).

God hates pride.

"The fear (reverence) of the Lord is to hate evil; pride and arrogance and the evil way and the perverted mouth, I hate" (Prov. 8:13).

"Everyone who is proud in heart is an abomination to the Lord; assuredly, he will not be unpunished" (Prov. 16:5).

God will not tolerate it in a person's heart and will break it.

"Whoever secretly slanders his neighbor, him I will destroy; no one who has a haughty look and an arrogant heart will I endure"(Ps. 101:5).

"The Lord will tear down the house of the proud, but He will establish the boundary of the widow" (Prov. 15:25).

Pride causes God to resist us.

"But God gives a greater grace. Therefore it says, 'God is opposed to the proud, but gives grace to the humble'" (Jas. 4:6).

It prevents and distracts us from focusing our thoughts on God.

"For the Lord is exalted, yet He regards the lowly, but the haughty He knows from afar" (Ps. 138:6).

He has to discipline us for pride.

"Pride goes before destruction and a haughty spirit before stumbling" (Prov. 16:18).

"Whoever exalts himself shall be humbled; and whoever humbles himself shall be exalted" (Matt. 23:12).

It leads to dishonor and shame.

"When pride comes, then comes dishonor, but with the humble is wisdom" (Prov. 11:2).

"But when his heart was lifted up and his spirit became so proud that he behaved arrogantly, he was deposed from his royal throne and his glory was taken away from him" (Dan. 5:20).

"A man's pride will bring him low, but a humble spirit will obtain honor" (Prov. 29:23).

God is trying to conform us to His own image. So when we are humble we receive grace, honor, and respect. Humility enables us to focus on reaching out in love to others and putting their needs above our own.

"Do nothing from selfishness or empty conceit, but with humility of mind regard one another as more important than yourselves" (Phil. 2:3).

"Love is patient, love is kind and is not jealous; love does not brag and is not arrogant, does act unbecomingly; it does not seek its own, is not provoked, does not take into account a wrong suffered, does not rejoice in unrighteousness, but rejoices with the truth; bears all things, believes all things, hopes all things, endures all things" (1 Cor. 13:4-7).

Here are some questions to ask ourselves to see if we have any evidence of pride:

Am I jealous when others are honored instead of me? ... Do I react or have difficulty accepting criticism? ... Am I quick to justify and defend myself when someone points out my faults? ... Do I compare myself with those around me? ... Do I trust in my own abilities, virtues, strengths, and resources? ... Do I have difficulty forgiving others? ... Do I have difficulty admitting I was wrong and asking for forgiveness? ... Do I think I am not a proud person? ... Do I complain or murmur? ... Am I more concerned about my reputation rather than God's? … Do I criticize, accuse, judge, or reject others? … Do I gossip or slander? … Do I hide behind sarcasm and joking at someone else's expense? … Do I feel sorry for myself because I am not appreciated? … Do I blame others for their failures? … Do I get concerned about what others think of me? … Do I desire to be successful apart from God's blessing or direction? … Do I refuse to give up what I perceive to be my personal rights? … Do I believe I am self-sufficient? … Do I look to others to serve me instead of being a servant myself? … Do I act or dress or talk in a way to draw attention to myself? … Am I competitive and get angry or pout when I don't win? … Do I have thoughts of suicide? … Do I think I can begin the day or make it through the day without communing with God? … Do I live for God's glory or my own pleasure and comfort?

Most people, after going through these questions, recognize areas of pride in their lives. Different people have different areas where pride tries to take up residence. Some pride is hidden. Some is obvious. Pride may deal with possessions, position, or attitudes about oneself. Whatever the area of pride in our lives, we need to ask Jesus to root it out and take it from us. God doesn't want His children to have pride.

Think about it:

1. What is the cause of pride?

2. What is the source and focus of pride?

3. Humbly ask God to show you any pride in your life and ask for and accept His forgiveness. Ask Him daily to help you recognize and root out any selfishness.

CHAPTER EIGHT

FORGIVENESS

Forgiveness is a supernatural act empowered by the Holy Spirit. It is a decision to let God be the Judge of any offense committed against us. Forgiveness is the core of Christianity. If there was one attitude, compassionate act, or motive that reflected the life of Christ, I believe it would be forgiveness.

We are commanded to forgive, **"Be kind and compassionate to one another, forgiving each other, just as in Christ, God forgave you"** (Eph. 4:32).

Many of us hold on to offenses because we believe that if we forgive we've let the offending person "off the hook." In failing to forgive, the only person who is "on the hook" is us. Unforgiveness is like drinking poison and hoping it will hurt the other person. It is possible to live with unforgiveness so long that we become blinded to its presence in our lives and it produces the fruit of bitterness. This fruit can be in the form of anger, resentment, hatred, ingratitude, a critical attitude, selfishness, sarcasm, slander, insensitivity to others, revenge, mistrust, or depression. It will defile us. It creates an open door for the enemy to damage our heart/spirit, soul, and body. Through a lifetime of unforgiveness many people become bitter and critical and their bodies dry up and waste away. We've all seen people like that. The only person they have harmed with their unforgiveness is themselves.

We have been told many lies which have convinced us to withhold forgiveness and feel justified in our bitterness and anger. "You don't have to forgive unless they apologize and ask for forgiveness" is probably the biggest lie about forgiveness that has enslaved people in bitterness and tormented them throughout their lives. This lie has its root in pride and asserts that we have certain rights and others must acquiesce to us. Forgiveness has nothing to do with what others owe us. It is our response to a request from God. What He asks of us He empowers us to do through the Holy Spirit. Only those who are followers of Christ have the ability to forgive from the heart, the very depths of the spirit, because the Spirit of God indwells and empowers us to do His will and obey His commands. God would never ask us to do something that was impossible to do. At His request and in His power we can forgive from the heart. We could never do it on our own.

When Jesus was dying on the cross He said, "**Father, forgive them for they do not know what they are doing**" (Lk. 23:34-35). When Stephen was being stoned, he asked the Lord, **"Do not hold this sin against them"** (Acts 7:59-60). Forgiveness means releasing the offender from the obligation to repay his debt and fully clearing his record. It is trusting in the death and resurrection of Jesus Christ as the payment for their sin. Forgiveness is not forgetting what was done to us. It is not excusing or tolerating sin. It is choosing not to take revenge. It is choosing to live with the consequences of another person's sin.

Suppose I go into a convenience store to get a pack of gum. While there some men come into the store to rob it, shoot me in the leg, run out, and are never caught or heard of again. Even if I have surgery, rehabilitation, and walk with a limp for the rest of my life, I must forgive the man who shot me. This may seem far-fetched, stretching for an example, but it happens every day. People hurt us, sometimes verbally or even physically. We are certainly often hurt emotionally. We can carry the wound through unforgiveness or let Jesus repair our hearts, rehabilitate us, and get us walking again through forgiveness. He will heal us. Our choice, our task, is to forgive. To forgive is to obey.

God is the only One who can forgive and forget. **"I will forgive their sin and I will remember it no more"** (Jer. 31:34). After we have forgiven from the heart with the power of the Holy Spirit, the offense will not come to mind as often as it did in the past. If someone asks us to remember the offense, we will be able to recall the event and many of the details, but with true forgiveness the pain of the offense, the emotional, hurting response, is not present anymore. The pain is gone and by that we know there has been true forgiveness. Before forgiveness we have the memory of the offense and the emotional pain. After forgiveness we have the memory of the offense but the pain is gone. That is the blessing of true forgiveness. God blesses us with a healing removal of the pain.

Forgiveness is not excusing the sin. The offender is still responsible for the pain and trauma they caused. However, it is God who holds them accountable, not us. God is the perfect Judge and will mete out justice perfectly to the offender. We can never give out perfect justice; God can.

There are many examples and teachings about forgiveness in the Word of God. We see Jesus and Stephen forgiving their executioners at the time of their deaths. Jesus teaches His disciples about forgiveness in Matthew 18:24-35. They asked Jesus if forgiving someone seven times is enough. His reply is that not only should they forgive someone seven times, but seventy times seven for the same sin in the same day. His meaning is clear; forgiveness is inexhaustible and unlimited.

In addition to forgiving other people, it is critical that we forgive ourselves. We can listen to the enemy's lies of condemnation and believe them about how wrong, stupid, or bad we are. However, this does not agree with God's Word about who we are and how He feels about us. **"There is no condemnation for those who are in Christ Jesus!"** (Rom. 8:1). We must confess our sin and release ourselves into God's merciful hands.

God is seeking tender, obedient, and merciful hearts like His, not hearts that are hardened. Hardened hearts block our relationship with God and harm the true intimacy He desires (Mt. 6:1-15; Ps. 103:1-2). With hearts that are hard, we prove that we do not trust Him to take care of every hurtful situation. The Holy Spirit is grieved when we don't forgive. Not only is He grieved by unforgiveness, the enemy is elated because he has been given the invitation/legal ground/right to torment us (Eph. 4:26-27; Matt. 18:34). Remember, unforgiveness is the largest open access for the enemy to come into our lives to harass and oppress us.

Here are some practical steps to help us forgive: Make a list of the people we need to forgive or feel negatively about, including ourselves. Write down what they did and the emotions it caused. God already knows if we are angry, bitter, or sad. Confess any sinful attitudes we have had toward that person. Ask God to help us forgive from our heart. Fully release these feelings and emotions. Believe that God has forgiven and will help us. He wants our hearts healed completely. God promises never to leave us or forsake us. Finally, we must ask God to bless the person who hurt us. Thank Him for His unconditional love and mercy. Commit to pray for them aloud every time the temptation comes to think negative thoughts about them. The enemy will see that the temptation isn't working and they will finally give up and leave us alone. Forgiveness is a major step toward freedom.

Think about it:

Here are some questions to help us measure whether we have forgiven someone who hurt us, be it a stranger or one we love:

1. Do I go out of my way to avoid that person?

2. Do I hope that the person is harmed or killed?

3. Do I gossip about, speak negatively about, or slander that person?

4. Have I asked God to forgive that person and thank Him for them?

5. Am I willing to ask God to bless that person?

CHAPTER NINE

SUFFERING

Perhaps the most painful question confronting a believer is the problem of suffering. Many people at some point in their lives question verbally or in their mind, "Why does a loving and wise God permit His children to suffer?" Or "Can I trust a God who allows His children to suffer?"

God, for His own reasons, gave all humans and angels "free will." We have the ability to choose to prove our love for Him by obeying Him. Being omniscient, knowing the past, present, and future in all things, He knew that most of us would reject Him. Still, He wanted to create something that was in His image that would choose to love and obey Him. That is more loving than creating robots that don't have the choice to obey. We are created for the sole purpose of glorifying Him. He lives for His own glory. He created for His own glory. He can do whatever He wants to, however and whenever He chooses to. He is God! And who are we to question His reasons? "Shall we accept blessings from God and not trouble?" Job asked. Later in Job 38-41, God asked, **"Where were you when I created ...."** In effect, He is saying "Do not assume that you can accept only what you understand or comprehend." Job had come to a wrong conclusion that suffering happens only to those who live impure lives. Yet God did not abandon him, but was there as Revealer, Comforter, Mediator, Savior, Strengthener, and Restorer.

In Isaiah 55: 8-9, God says "**'For My thoughts are not your thoughts, nor are your ways My ways,' says the Lord. 'For as the heavens are higher than the earth, so are My ways higher than your ways and My thoughts than your thoughts.'**"

What keeps us going is the faith/confidence we have in the character and nature of God. He is completely sovereign. Everything that happens, good or bad, is under His control. God is still God and we are still not God. Because Jesus Himself was betrayed and suffered, He is able to intercede for us. Job and Joseph were given glimpses of what it is to stand in the place of an intercessor to forgive and restore friends and family.

We live in a fallen world because of the choices made by Lucifer, Adam, and Eve to disobey God. We must understand and accept the truth that suffering, death, disease, pain, and sorrow are all part of this life for the righteous and unrighteous. Suffering is a process in the framework of time in which God does the healing. Time does not heal. Often, we react to the pain and want relief. Pain is a reminder that we live in a fallen world and a consequence to turn our attention toward God.

There are several causes of suffering:

1. Natural consequence of our own sin or disobedience to God's laws.

2. A result of the sins of others, such as war, injustice, slander, gossip, or abuse.

3. Self-inflicted from emotional stress, unforgiveness, bad health habits, and some diseases.

4. A result of trauma such as storms, floods, earthquakes, and epidemics.

5. The result of persecution for the sake of righteousness.

We must ask God for discernment to determine why we suffer. We can suffer because of our position or disposition. Peter brings this out in his first epistle: **"Servants, be submissive to your masters with all respect, not only to those who are good and gentle but also to those who are unreasonable. For this finds favor, if for the sake of conscience toward God a man bears up under sorrows when suffering unjustly"** (1 Pet. 2:18-19).

God does not cause suffering. He allows it and uses it for His purposes. When He disciplines us for our sin, it is motivated by His perfect love. **"He is a gracious, compassionate God, slow to anger and abundant in loving kindness, and one who relents concerning calamity"** (Job 4:2).

And yet, we ask, what is the purpose of suffering?

1. To glorify God

Our ultimate purpose in life is to bring God glory and

to give a correct estimate or opinion of who He is.

"**As He passed by, He saw a man blind from birth. And His disciples asked Him, 'Rabbi, who sinned, this man or his parents, that he would be born blind?' Jesus answered 'It was neither that this man sinned, nor his parents; but it was so that the works of God might be displayed in him'**" (Jn. 9:1-3).

Mary and Martha said about Lazarus, "**Lord, behold he whom you love is sick. But when Jesus heard this, He said, 'This sickness is not to end in death, but for the glory of God, so that the Son of God may be glorified by it'**" (Jn. 11:3-4).

Paul reminded the Corinthians, "**We are afflicted in every way, but not crushed; perplexed, but not despairing; persecuted, but not forsaken; struck down, but not destroyed ... so that the grace which is spreading to more and more people may cause the giving of thanks to abound to the glory of God**" (2 Cor. 4:7-15).

2. To make us like Jesus

The sufferings we endure here are a continuation of the tribulations Christ endured on earth. He is the Head of the body of believers, so He suffers when we suffer.

"**Now I rejoice in my sufferings for your sake, and in my flesh I do my share on behalf of His body, which is the church, in filling up what is lacking in Christ's afflictions**" (Col. 1:24).

"'**Saul, Saul, why are you persecuting Me?' And he said, 'Who are You, Lord?' And He said, 'I am Jesus whom you are persecuting, but get up and enter the city, and it will be told you what you must do'**" (Acts 9:4-5, 22:7-8).

"**In all their affliction He was afflicted and the angel**

of His presence saved them; In His love and in His mercy He redeemed them, and He lifted them and carried them all the days of old" (Isa. 63:9). "That I may know Him, and the power of His resurrection and the fellowship of His sufferings, being conformed to His death" (Phil. 3:10).

Many people are shocked when they suffer and fight against it, all the while knowing others suffer, but believing they can escape it. Some suffering, that is the result of our sin, we can escape when we are obedient.

"Beloved, do not be surprised at the fiery ordeal among you, which comes upon you for your testing, as though some strange thing were happening to you; but to the degree that you share the sufferings of Christ, keep on rejoicing, so that also at the revelation of His glory you may rejoice with exultation. If you are reviled for the name of Christ, you are blessed, because the Spirit of glory and of God rests on you. Make sure that none of you suffers as a murderer, or thief, or evildoer, or a troublesome meddler; but if anyone suffers as a Christian, he is not to be ashamed, but is to glorify God in this name" (1 Pet. 4:12-16).

A silversmith knows when silver is pure by looking into it. He continues heating and purifying it until he sees a perfect image of himself. "Perfect," according to the Greek, means "complete, fully qualified."

"You have tried us, O God; You have refined us as silver is refined" (Ps. 66:10).

"The refining pot is for silver and the furnace for gold, but the Lord tests hearts" (Prov. 17:3).

"And not only this, but we also exult in our tribulations, knowing that tribulation brings about perseverance; and perseverance, proven character; and proven character, hope; and hope does not disappoint because the love of God has been poured out within our hearts through the Holy Spirit who was given to us" (Rom. 5:3-5).

3. To test us to prove us strong and faithful
  When we go through trials and our faith remains strong, it proves to us and to others Who He is and Whose we are. The evidence of faith is cheerful obedience! See Hebrews 11 and 1 Samuel 15.
  "Examine me, O Lord, and try me; test my mind and my heart" (Ps. 26:2).
  "But He knows the way I take; when He has tried me, I shall come out as gold" (Job 23:10).

4. To refine our lives and teach us dependence
  Abraham passed the test God gave him and was blessed (Gen. 22:1-2, 15-18).
  "Even in this you greatly rejoice, though now for a little while, if necessary, you have been distressed by various trials, so that the proof of your faith, being more precious than gold which is perishable, even though tested by fire, may be found to result in praise and glory and honor at the revelation of Jesus Christ" (1 Pet. 1:6-7).
  Confidence in our flesh is a lack of faith. Affliction can turn our attention toward God.
  "And He has said to me, 'My grace is sufficient for you, for power is perfected in weakness' (verse 9) ... Therefore, I am well content with weaknesses, with insults, with distresses, with persecutions, with difficulties, for Christ's sake; for when I am weak, then I am strong" (verse 10) (2 Cor. 12:1-10).

"I will go away and return to My place until they
acknowledge their guilt and seek my face; in their affliction
they will earnestly seek Me" (Hos. 5:15).

"Before I was afflicted I went astray, but now I keep
Your word. It is good for me that I was afflicted, that I may
learn Your statutes" (Ps. 119:67, 71).

Without suffering, there would be neither full growth
nor fruitfulness. Nothing God allows is accidental or without
design.

"Jesus said, 'I am the true vine, and My father is
the vinedresser. Every branch in Me that does not bear
fruit, He takes away; and every branch that bears fruit, He
prunes so that it may bear more fruit'" (Jn. 15:1-2).

5. To rid us of pride and teach us humility

God hates pride and will not tolerate it. He allows us
to choose. We either humble ourselves with His help or He
will allow us to suffer the consequences in order for us to be
humbled so He can be in our presence.

"The fear (reverence) of the Lord is to hate evil;
pride and arrogance and the evil way and the perverted
mouth, I hate" (Prov. 8:13).

"But He gives a greater grace. Therefore it says God
is opposed to the proud, but gives grace to the humble"
(Jas. 4:6).

"And whoever exalts himself shall be humbled; and
whoever humbles himself shall be exalted" (Matt. 23:12).

6. To produce fruit

If we allow suffering to accomplish its purpose, it can bring:

Patience/endurance – "For you have need of

endurance, so that when you have done the will of God, you may receive what was promised" (Heb. 10:36).

"Consider it all joy, my brethren, when you encounter various trials, knowing that the testing of your faith produces endurance" (Jas. 1:2-3).

Joy – "For his anger is but for a moment, His favor is for a lifetime; weeping may last for the night, but a shout of joy comes in the morning" (Ps. 30:5).

"Those who sow in tears shall reap with joyful shouting ..." (Ps. 126:5).

Knowledge – "Blessed is the man whom You chasten, O Lord, And whom You teach out of Your law" (Ps. 94:12).

Maturity – "After you have suffered for a little while, the God of all grace, Who called you to His eternal glory in Christ, will Himself perfect, confirm, and establish you" (1 Pet. 5:8).

7. To rebuke our sin and discipline us because He loves us

"For what credit is there if, when you sin and are harshly treated, you endure it with patience? But if when you do what is right and suffer for it and you patiently endure it, this finds favor with God" (1 Pet. 2:20).

"For it is better, if God should will it so, that you suffer for doing what is right rather than for doing what is wrong" (1 Pet. 3:17).

"My son, do not reject the discipline of the Lord or hate His reproof, for whom the Lord loves He reproves, even as a father corrects the son in whom he delights" (Prov. 3:11-12).

"For our earthly fathers disciplined us for a short time as seemed best to them, but He disciplines us for our

good, so that we may share His holiness. All discipline for the moment seems not to be joyful, but sorrowful; yet to those who have been trained by it, afterwards it yields the peaceful fruit of righteousness" (Heb. 12:10-11).

8. To silence the devil

Satan once accused Job of merely serving God for the material blessings involved. But the Lord allowed the devil to torment Job to demonstrate that His servant loved Him because of who He was, not for what he could get from Him (Job 1:9-12, 2:3-7).

9. To present us with opportunities

Suffering has been used to spread the gospel and complete the work of Christ. Paul and Silas praying and singing in prison was a powerful testimony resulting in the conversion of the jailer and his family (Acts 16:23-33).

Paul explained that his fellow minister, Epaphroditus, nearly died of an illness for the work of Christ, risking his life to complete his service to Paul. The Philippians were to receive him with joy and hold men like him in high regard (Phil. 2:25-30).

10. To enlarge our ministry toward others

When we turn to Him, receive His comfort, and rest in His arms, we will be comforted. Then we can give it to others. Each of us has a special place in strengthening the body of Christ.

"Blessed be the God and Father of our Lord Jesus Christ, the Father of mercies and God of all comfort, who comforts us in all our affliction so that we will be able to

comfort those who are in any affliction with the comfort with which we ourselves are comforted by God" (2 Cor. 1:3-4).

"Simon, Simon, behold, Satan has demanded permission to sift you like wheat; but I have prayed for you, that your faith may not fail; and you, when once you have turned again, strengthen your brothers" (Lk. 22:31-32).

11. To put trials into God's perspective – to see it from His viewpoint

When we see our current trials compared to His future glory, we can rejoice in the middle of them. This is not the feeling of happiness. It is deep, abiding joy! And it prepares us to reign with Him later.

"We ought always to give thanks to God for you, brethren, as is only fitting, because your faith is greatly enlarged, and the love of each one of you toward one another grows ever greater; therefore, we ourselves speak proudly of you among the churches of God for your perseverance and faith in the midst of all your persecutions and afflictions which you endure. This is a plain indication of God's righteous judgment so that you will be considered worthy of the kingdom of God, for which indeed you are suffering" (2 Thess. 1:3-5).

"For our momentary, light affliction is producing for us an eternal weight of glory far beyond all comparison, while we look not at the things which are seen, for the things which are seen are temporal, but the things which are not seen are eternal" (2 Cor. 4:17-18).

"The Spirit Himself testifies with our spirit that we are children of God, and if children, heirs also, heirs of God and fellow heirs with Christ if indeed we suffer with

Him so that we may also be glorified with Him" (Rom. 8:16-18).

"If we endure, we will also reign with Him; If we deny Him, He also will deny us; If we are faithless, He remains faithful, for He cannot deny Himself" (2 Tim. 2:12-13).

Suffering is like a two-sided coin. On one side, it is allowed by God for all of the above reasons. The other side of the coin is that Satan attempts to use suffering to bring out the worst in us.

"Let no one say when he is tempted, 'I am being tempted by God'; for God cannot be tempted by evil, and He Himself does not tempt anyone. But each one is tempted when he is carried away and enticed by his own lust. Then when lust has conceived, it gives birth to sin; and when sin is accomplished, it brings forth death. Do not be deceived, my beloved brethren. Every good thing given and every perfect gift is from above, coming down from the Father of light, with whom there is no variation or shifting shadow" (Jas. 1:13-14).

As believers, we can respond to suffering in at least three different ways:

1. *Treat it too lightly* as Esau did his birthright (Heb. 12:5, 16). Numbered, bolded, underlined like the ones just previous.

2. *Be afraid of the pain, treat it too seriously, and faint under it.* To be crushed, depressed, or despairing will give a negative testimony about God. This is about giving up on God and listening to the lies of the enemy, e.g. that suicide is the solution to free us from the pain. Suicide is about pride (self-pity),

RELEASED

selfishness, murder, cruelty to family and friends left behind, and lack of trust in God. It is saying God isn't big enough or cares enough to be with me and get me through the trial and pain. See 2 Corinthians 5:7-15 and Job 4, 5:7. It is vital to stay focused on God and His promises, not the circumstances. Peter walked on water with his eyes on Jesus, but when he took his eyes off of Jesus, he sank. God commands us not to be afraid over 140 times in His Word.

3. Be exercised by it, which means to receive instruction from it. It's about trusting God. This is the reaction He desires (Heb.13:11-13). Both Peter and Paul told us to commit our pain and suffering to God, realizing He is faithful to work out all things for good and for His glory for those who love and serve Him (Rom. 8:28; 1 Pet. 4:19). James tells us to **"count it all joy when we experience these dark hours"** (Jas. 1:2). This can be done only in the power of the Holy Spirit Who gives us comfort and strength! He inhabits the praises of His people. One way we can shut the enemy up and draw God's presence to us is to sing praises to Him in the midst of our suffering. It is not about how we feel. It's about obedience.

As David said in Psalms 28:7 and 61:2-4, the Lord is our only source of strength, our rock, our refuge, and shelter. The battle belongs to the Lord and our job is to stand firm and totally rely on Him (Eph. 6:10-12). Ask God to reveal the source or cause of the suffering. He will give us the strength and patience to endure it so we can be more than conquerors! (Rom. 8:37). Take courage in remembering what the apostle Paul said, **"For I consider that the sufferings of this present time are not worthy to be compared with the glory that is to be revealed to us"** (Rom. 8:18).

120

Think about it

1. How have you responded to your suffering?

2. Jesus learned obedience through His suffering. What are some of the things you have learned through yours?

PART FOUR:

RELEASED –
A PRISONER NO MORE

CHAPTER TEN

IDENTIFYING AND WEAKENING
THE ENEMY

Regaining lost territory is a process. Closing doors we have opened to the enemy and taking away his legal ground to harass and torment us is a spiritual process. The ministry God has allowed us to participate in is dedicated to helping Christians regain lost territory and be freed from the snares of the enemy: to set the prisoners free. Finding freedom is best done with mature Christians who are experienced in ministering deliverance. The word "deliverance" sometimes brings to mind scary, spooky stuff. Images flash in our minds of swooping demons with flashing, fanged teeth putting up a grand battle with smoke and fire to keep the one they have possessed. That's precisely the picture the enemy wants us to have and, thanks to Hollywood, most of us have those images in our heads.

But deliverance is neither spooky nor scary. In fact, it is freeing. Another image of deliverance is that of the person being delivered rolling on the floor, screaming, and yelling obscenities. Sorry if this is disillusioning, but that doesn't happen often either. Deliverance is a spiritual process of confessing (agreeing with God) any sin we have committed and any part we have had in opening the door to the enemy.

Next, deliverance is prayer. We pray, asking God to forgive us and strengthen us through the Holy Spirit so we will not repeat sinful behavior. When we have confessed, repented, and received forgiveness from our Loving Father, the enemy is weakened and has no more legal right to harass us. He is then told to leave in the name of Jesus Christ by the power of the Holy Spirit, and he must go.

Who are these enemies that must leave? Besides Satan, the evil spirits that are harassing us have names. Most of the time, the actual names of the individual spirits are difficult to understand and pronounce. They are more easily identified by their assignment: Fear, Pride, and Infirmity, for example. Each wicked angel has an assignment. They know and are identified by their assignment. We know their assignment name by what they have done or are trying to do to us. The following are the identities and assignments of evil spirits. Below the name or assignment are the symptoms of harassment by an evil spirit through an open door. Remember, we give the enemy the "legal right" to harass, oppress, and torment us when we have an open door. Those open doors are: Willful Disobedience, Unforgiveness, Inherited Iniquities, Trauma, Inner Vows and Judgments, and Careless Invasion of Enemy Territory.

Take a look at this list and identify the enemy that is harassing you -- what they are doing and causing in your life. Take note: not all of the following symptoms in your life are caused by evil spirits. Those shown here may be caused by wicked angels, but our response to things happening in our lives may open the door for them to come in as well. For example, diabetes may not be caused by the spirit of infirmity, BUT my response to having diabetes, like self-pity, impatience, irritability, self-doubts, doubts about God loving me, etc., may open the door for the enemy to use diabetes to oppress and/or torment me.

Many ministries have compiled lists of spirits and their symptoms. We have also compiled these lists and made changes based on our eleven years of observation and experience in deliverance ministry.

The spirit of confusion/error – 1 Jn. 4:6; 2 Pet. 3:17; Jas. 4:13-18, 5:19-20; 1 Cor. 12:33

- Compromise
- Confusion
- Continuous wrong decisions
- Cults
- Continual forgetfulness
- Doubt
- False teachers
- False tongues
- False prophets and preachers
- Gender confusion
- Illiteracy
- Indifference
- Immaturity
- Inappropriate thinking or behavior
- Intellectualism
- Irresponsibility
- Mental illness

- Mind control, blocking
- Procrastination
- Soul fragmenting
- Unbelief

The spirit of bondage/idolatry – Rom. 8:15; Heb. 2:15

- Alcohol
- Anorexia
- Addicted to another person/codependency
- Addicted to a specific sin
- Addicted to possessions
- Blocked (emotions, affections, etc.)
- Bulimia
- Chance – getting something for nothing
- Cigarettes
- Driving too fast
- Drugs (legal and illegal)
- Computers (games, chat rooms, etc.)
- Food (sweets, junk, gluttony)
- Financial bondage
- Frigidity
- Gambling
- Materialism/possessions
- Racism
- Pornography
- Perfectionism
- Sex
- Soul ties (physical, emotional, sexual)
- Stealing

- Superiority
- Television
- Workaholic

The spirit of Jezebel (control and rebellion) – 1 Kings 21; Isa. 30:1; 1 Sam. 12:15, 15:23-24; Ps. 68:6; 1 Tim.6:1; Rev. 2:20-28

- Anger
- Bitterness
- Bossy
- Competitive
- Controlling
- Critical
- Deceitful
- Deliberate disobedience
- Disrespectful attitude
- Discouraging
- Discrediting
- Dominates
- Endless demands
- False humility
- Fearful
- Habitually "forgetting"
- Frowns
- Independence
- Insecure
- Insinuation
- Legalism
- Manipulates

- Negative
- Nagging
- Not submit to authority
- Pretense
- Pouting
- Prideful
- Rage
- Rebellion
- Religious
- Resentment
- Ritualism
- Sarcasm
- Self-promotion
- Self pity
- Sighs
- Silent treatment
- Sneers
- Socialism
- Stubborn, wants own way
- Temper

The spirit of deaf and dumb – Mk. 9:25-27; Lk. 9:42; Mt. 12:22

- Abortion
- Accidents with water- drowning
- Accidents with fire
- Autism (in some cases)
- Convulsions
- Deafness

- Diseases of the eyes and ears
- Epilepsy
- Grinding of the teeth
- Insanity
- Madness
- Murder
- Seizures
- Schizophrenia
- Stupor
- Suicide attempts, tendencies

The spirit of divination – (Lev. 20:27; Deut. 7:25-26; Ex. 22:18; 1 Sam. 15:23, 28:5-19; Isa. 47:13-14; Mic. 5:12; Acts 16:16-18; Rev. 21:8)

- Astrology
- Automatic writing
- Channeling
- Charms
- Crystal balls
- Demonic/ witchcraft and games, movies, books
- Drugs
- Eastern religions
- Familiar spirits
- Freemasonry and other secret organizations
- Fortune tellers
- Horoscopes
- Hypnosis
- Indian witchcraft medicine men
- Independence
- Levitation

- Manipulation
- Mysticism
- Ouija boards
- Palm readers
- Rebellion and stubbornness
- Satanism (worship of Satan)
- Séances
- Tarot cards
- TM (transcendental meditation)
- Voodoo
- Witching/divining
- Worship of the dead

The spirit of haughtiness/pride – Prov. 6:16-17; Prov. 16:18-19; Is. 14:14; Ez. 16:49-50

- Accusing
- Arguments
- Arrogance
- Bragging
- Controlling
- Constant criticism
- Contention
- Dictatorial
- Domineering
- Egotistical
- Faultfinding
- Gossip
- Habitually late
- Mockery/scorn/making fun/put downs
- Independence

- Intellectualism
- Judgment
- Prejudice
- Pride
- Rudeness
- Quarreling/strife
- Sarcasm
- Self-righteousness
- Self-pity
- Stubbornness
- Superiority
- Vanity

The spirit of heaviness – Isa. 61:3

- Abnormal mourning
- Broken heartedness
- Continual sorrow/sadness
- Defilement
- Depression
- Despair
- Discouragement
- Gloominess
- Hopelessness
- Humiliation
- Loneliness
- Rejection
- Sadness
- Self-pity
- Shame
- Unjustified guilt

- Whining
- Wounded spirit

The spirit of infirmity – Lk. 13:11; I Cor. 11:27-30; Acts 10:38

- Allergies
- Arthritis
- Cancer
- Diabetes
- Disorders of the body that linger
- Female problems
- Fevers
- Fungus
- Heart disease
- High blood pressure
- Tension headache
- Weakness and feebleness

The spirit of jealousy – Num. 5:14; Gen. 37:3-11; Prov. 10:12

- Abortion
- Betrayal
- Builds protective walls
- Covetousness
- Cruelty
- Distrustfulness
- Feeling of being less loved by God than other people

- Divorce
- Division
- Fears God loves others more
- Insecurity
- Irrational anger, wrath, rage
- Hatred
- Jealousy
- Revenge
- Self-centeredness
- Suspicion
- Unnatural competition

The spirit of lying – 1 Kings 22:23; 2 Chron. 18:22; Matt. 12:36; Jn. 8:44; Eph. 4:25; 1 Thess. 2:9; 1 Tim. 4:7; 2 Pet. 2:1-2

- Accusation
- Condemnation
- Exaggeration
- Excessive talking
- Daydreaming
- Deception
- Emotionalism
- Flattery
- Insecure/inferior
- Intimidation
- Lying about God, self or others (ex. "God doesn't love me or doesn't care," "I will never change" "I will never get married" etc.)
- Performance
- Poor self image

("I am ugly, dumb, stupid, worthless, liar, fat, etc.)
- Profanity
- Religious spirit (legalism)
- Shame
- Shyness, timidity
- Strong delusions
- Unworthy
- Vain imaginations

The spirit of perverseness – Isa. 5:20, 19:14; Rom. 1:26-32; 2 Cor. 10:5

- Abnormal crankiness
- All sexual deviations
- Continually irritable
- False teachers/false doctrine
- Error
- Homosexuality/gender confusion
- Multi-partner sex orgies
- Polygamy
- Sadomasochism
- Self-lovers
- Sexual deviations
- Twisted thinking
- Occult
- Twisting God's Word to Satan's advantage
- Unreasonableness

The spirit of stupor (slumber/sleep) – Isa. 29:10; Rom. 11:8

- Blocks success
- Wish had not been born
- Constant fatigue
- Despondent
- Draws back from life, human spirit is asleep
- Insomnia
- Laziness
- Lethargy
- Passivity
- Procrastination
- Sleepiness

The spirit of antichrist – (1 Jn. 4:3-6, 2:22; 2 Jn. 2:7-10)

- Atheism
- Attempts to replace Christ
- Blasphemes the Holy Spirit and His gifts
- Causes church splits
- Condemnation of the Word
- Gives up on Christianity
- Harasses, martyrs, and persecutes the saints
- Explains away all the power of God in the life of a saint (no miracles)
- Opposes the Bible, Christ's deity and humanity
- Rationalized the Word
- Ministry/ministers are suppressed
- Seduces one to error

The spirit of whoredom – Hos. 4:12, 5:4; I Cor. 6:12-20; I

Jn. 2:15-17; Phil. 3:18-19; 1 Tim. 6:7-12; Rom. 8:12-14

- Adultery
- Anything worshipped or trusted in for security
- Bestiality
- Exhibitionism
- Fornication
- Harlotry/prostitute
- Idolatry
- Illegitimacy
- Incest
- Love of money
- Love of social standing
- Love of the world
- Lust of the flesh
- Lust for position
- Masturbation
- Molestation
- Multi-partner sex
- Peeping tom
- Pornography
- Placing anyone or anything before God
- Rape
- Seduction
- Voyeurism

Finally, we look at the spirit of fear. Not everyone will be affected by all the spirits we have listed. Some may have infirmity and bondage. Others may have whoredom, lying, or haughtiness/pride. But we have never met anyone who has not been affected by the spirit of fear. Fear is the spirit that introduces the other spirits to us. For example, we may sin sexually. The spirit of fear will try to keep it quiet for FEAR we will be shunned or ridiculed. The spirit of fear will bring in the lying spirit so that we will try to cover up the sin. The spirit of bondage will be introduced to tempt us to continue in that sin. They all work together, but it was fear that set us up.

The spirit of fear – Job 3:25; Ps. 23:4, 27:1, 91:4-5, 112:7-8; Prov. 29:25; Is. 41:10, 54:14; Lk. 12:32; Rom. 8:15; Heb. 13:5-6; 2 Tim. 1:7; 1 Jn. 4:18

- Abandonment by God
- Abandonment by people
- Accidents
- Allergies
- Animals
- Authority figures
- Becoming a homosexual
- Being inferior
- Being left alone
- Committing suicide
- Committed the unpardonable sin
- Confrontation
- Crossing bridges
- Crowds
- Dark
- Death or dying
- Death of a loved one
- Dogs
- Disease
- Disapproval

- Divorce
- Driving
- Drowning
- Embarrassment
- Enclosed spaces
- Evil spirits
- Failure
- Fire
- Flying in an airplane
- Financial problems
- Future
- Getting fat
- Germs
- Getting caught
- Getting angry or violent
- Grocery stores
- Heights
- Hurting loved ones
- Inadequacy
- Inability to cope
- Injury
- Losing control
- Losing your mind
- Losing possessions
- Losing salvation
- Loud noises
- Intimate relationships
- Malls
- Marriage
- Marriage breakup
- Men

- Mice
- Over eating
- Nightmares
- Never getting married
- Not being loved
- Old age
- Open or public places
- Opinions of others
- Over spending
- Pain
- Past being found out
- Physical abuse
- Poverty
- Public speaking
- Rape
- Rejection
- Ridicule
- Satan
- Snakes
- Sexual abuse
- Spiders or bugs
- Sin being exposed
- Swimming
- Storms
- Success
- Terminal illness
- Theft
- Verbal abuse
- Victimized by crime
- Violence
- Water

- Women

If you are a Christian living a defeated life, in bondage to sin, confused, and have no peace, you are most probably being harassed by the enemy. If you feel despondent, dejected, and hopeless, then you are likely being tormented by him. He will try to make you think everything that is wrong with you is your fault, that it's all in your mind, and that you're cracking up. He doesn't want you to know you are being oppressed and tormented. The goal is to make you a prisoner. You are saved, but you can't minister, encourage, or build up. If this is the case, and your job, your family, and your life are falling apart, you can't change anyone else, but you can let Jesus change you. The Lord Jesus Christ will heal you, free you, and deliver you from the bonds of the enemy. You need to seek help today.

Think about it:

1. Read John 10:10. Do you believe that Jesus Christ came to give you an abundant life of peace and joy even here on earth?

2. Are there any disadvantages to having Jesus Christ heal your past so that you can live peacefully in the present?

3. Who wants you to be free?

4. Who doesn't want you to be free?

CHAPTER ELEVEN

INNER HEALING

There is an aspect of deliverance called Inner Healing that is getting more attention these days. Some who minister deliverance have been familiar with it for years, and many have either ignored it or were not aware of it. Inner Healing is a part of deliverance wherein the Holy Spirit makes us aware of the lies we have believed regarding an event or series of events which led to an open door. The enemy has taken this event or events and lied to us about them. For example, if I was molested as a child, the enemy would immediately put some lie thoughts into my head. These lies may sound like the following statements.

"I let them do this to me, so it's my fault."

"God doesn't care about me or He wouldn't have let this happen."

"I'll never again trust those in authority over me as long as I live."

In Inner Healing, Jesus replaces the lies we have believed with the truth. He shines the light of truth on those lies by telling us what really happened, what He thinks of what happened, and what He really thinks of us.

Like the other parts of deliverance, Inner Healing should be handled by mature Christians who are experienced in ministering Inner Healing. Original lies based on trauma are deep-seated and usually begin when we are very young. If we buy into a lie of the enemy when we're young it will affect us throughout our lives and have a bearing on all of our relationships.

Following are the testimonies of some sweet, wonderful, yet wounded Christians to whom we have ministered. The names have been changed to protect their identity.

Sherrie's testimony:

Sherrie's dad was wounded in early childhood. He made money his idol and hoarded it. He put it before his family and misused it. He was fearful because he had gone without food and clothing as a child. When he punished Sherrie, he was abusive. His wounded heart did not know how to change or how to be healed. One time he was drunk, molested her, and begged her not to tell her mother. Her trust in him as her authority was destroyed and a spirit of confusion took over her mind.

At age three, Sherrie was molested by a man who was supposed to be a friend of the family and his wife told her it was her fault. Her parents had entrusted her and her brother to this couple to babysit them at their home. The Lord blocked this memory for her protection until later adult years, but she felt confused, alone, and very fearful.

Sherrie's mother was in such emotional pain that she

was detached emotionally, and again Sherri put up a wall to protect herself. She believed the lie that her mother hated her. Later, feelings of anger, resentment, fear, bitterness, and depression set in as strongholds.

She trusted boyfriends only to have them abandon or betray her. When she married John, she believed "this is a man who will never hurt me." She didn't know he was also wounded, and was again disappointed.

She was angry at God for allowing the abuse. Through deliverance and inner healing, she learned that God hurts and is sad when His children are mistreated. He reassured Sherrie that all people are given free will and the ones who listen to the enemy's flagrant lies and believe them can be cruel to each other. Because God understands, she knows she was not alone. He was there and saw it all. She accepts this as truth from Jesus Christ.

When Jesus freed her from all the anger, bitterness, lies, and confusion and spoke His truth to her spirit about all the abusers and herself, she was able to forgive them all and be fully healed. Her trust in God was restored. Later her daughter said, "I praise God for His mighty work in my Mama! She is full of joy and peace for the first time in her life. She talked about how loved she is. She carries herself differently today and has truly been made a new creation, full of the Spirit." Her marriage is healing and she has compassion on others as she ministers now to them. She knows Jesus Christ is the great physician and Healer.

Susan's Testimony:

Susan grew up in a Christian home with a perfectionist,

controlling dad who had occasional outbursts of anger. Her mother was fearful, critical, and coveted and collected material things she didn't need. Both parents suffered with depression. Fear and depression passed down to Susan and even to her children. Negative words had been spoken against her and her husband. She also spoke them against her husband. He was wounded and did not feel respected.

As a child, peers at school were cruel, ostracized her, and betrayed her many times. She believed the lie that "something must be wrong with me." She was attractive and kind and did not provoke these attacks. She felt inferior, rejected, embarrassed, and alone. Some boys had taken advantage of her innocence and selfishly tried to prey on her for gratification of their own lust. The lie entered her mind to mistrust everyone, especially God. She made inner vows. All of this played out in her mind and in the intimacy in her marriage. Financial problems loomed for several years and she resented that her husband didn't make more money. She worked full time and wanted to be home. Her security was in owning a house. He made efforts to prove the negative words spoken against him about his lack of financial provision were not true. She suffered with depression, had thoughts of suicide, and her boss told her to take a leave of absence. She entered a mental health hospital and was medicated, but still was immobilized with fear and didn't want to leave her house. She could multitask in the past, but now could only barely do one simple task each day.

After the Holy Spirit helped her work through forgiveness of everyone in her past, including herself, she felt a lifting she had never known before. Jesus healed her painful memories, exposed the lies, and gave her His truth. He healed her mind and emotions. She began to believe her identity and value in Christ. She is learning not to worry but to rest, be at peace, and trust Jesus. She learned she cannot control others or her circumstances. Her fear was paralyzing her. The confusion was lifted and the clarity of her mind was evident. She is learning to speak life and truth to herself, husband, and children. Jesus changed her from handwringing anxiety and heaviness to light-hearted, confident, and peaceful. She is eager for everyone else who is wounded to be free, too!

George's Testimony:

George grew up in a home where church attendance was sporadic. His mother was the caregiver and his dad was a strict perfectionist, fearful and angry, and suffered from depression. He was very driven and unkind to his wife and children. Performance and competition became his idol stemming from a root of fear and pride.

George suffered from fear of failure, others' opinions, inadequacy, and got angry often. He believed God was like his dad in the area of shaming. He made an inner vow, "I will never be like my dad." He carried this vow along with unforgiveness until his middle forties. He was on medication for depression and at times became immobilized with fear at his job. He believed the lie that if he acted more like Jesus, motivating his employees out of love instead of anger, they would take advantage of him and not respect him. So he lost his temper regularly in public and yelled at his employees. Some of them lost respect for him. He did not get his identity from Christ but in the lies he believed about others and his own performance. His pride was also involved as he believed his employees' performance was a reflection of him. He was indeed acting very much like his dad in his rage, the very thing he had vowed not to do. He was robbed of peace and joy.

The Lord helped him to forgive his dad and himself. Jesus imparted to him the truth that George was His cherished prize and treasure. He values George's heart and is not looking at his performance.

Now, on his job he can have peace without fear. His wife said he is very changed, is not anxious, and has peace. In compassion, he now refers others to receive ministry. He is free and wants others to experience freedom!

John's Testimony:

John grew up in a home with a loving, supportive, and encouraging mother. They were very close. However, his dad was a fearful, critical, negative, perfectionist and was not affectionate. He was also addicted to pornography and angry. He was driven and pressured John in athletics. He hadn't had a dad to raise him, so he didn't know how to be a father to John.

When John was in kindergarten he went swimming and an older boy made fun of his private parts in front of thirty other children. He felt confused, ashamed, and exposed. The lie that entered his mind was "something is wrong with me."

John was driven in athletics and making good grades in order to get his dad's attention and approval. Like his dad, he also had an addiction to pornography and anger that started at age twelve. Performance and control became his idols. In his teen years, he was wounded by negative words from a girl who said he was short. Other peers made fun of him for being short. This hurt him and he grew angry and bitter. He bought and wore shoe raisers to appear taller. The theme of rejection continued. He experienced more rejection from girls and struggled to be popular. Being popular became an idol.

He was betrayed by a girlfriend and became jealous and controlling when the relationship ended in a fight that went to court. He said, "She was my life." He realized his pride and anger issues. Fears of being inadequate, inferior, and rejected were magnified and further embedded.

More of the lies he believed were "You'll never find a wife on fire for God" and "My life is boring and will never change." He feared marriage and failure.

He became withdrawn, isolated, depressed, and listened to and believed negative lies in his mind. Pride was firmly rooted in the form of self-pity and the need to be right and in control. His relationship with and trust in God was damaged.

Through deliverance, he made a decision to forgive everyone who wounded him. He also forgave himself. Jesus uprooted the lies and shined the light of His truth for John. He learned deep in his heart and spirit that he was wonderfully created, that he belongs to Jesus, and that nothing is wrong with him. He embraced that truth and is peaceful, free, and doing very well in medical school.

Matt's testimony:

Matt trusted Christ as his Savior at age 12. His home life was very difficult. He had a deep respect for his dad who he said was kind and supportive, but was orphaned and did not know how to get involved in Matt's life. Matt felt abandoned and had no one to lead or direct him. His father became an alcoholic, workaholic, and physically abusive to Matt's mother. He would get drunk and leave home for days at a time. His mother was also verbally and physically abusive to his dad. Both parents committed adultery. In later years, they came to Christ but did not attend church or follow Him.

Matt was a teenager when he found pornography, and his parents told him to just keep it hidden. The anger and pornography became strongholds as he believed the lie that this would give him comfort. Since age 15, he vowed he would never be alone. He committed fornication dozens of times. He said, "I had no respect for women." Lies entered with thoughts of inferiority, helplessness, self-pity, loneliness, inadequacy, anxiety, intense fears of being left alone, rejection, and abandonment. He stole things at work and lied. He had road rage and control issues. Searching for comfort and identity, he was selfish, miserable, lonely, and carried a load of guilt and heaviness.

At a young age, Matt married Julie and it ended soon after. Then Matt married Cathy and had children only to have her leave him. Deep depression set in when thinking of losing his wife and children. Later, he married Jane who also left and then divorced him. His dad died suddenly and then his mom died a few weeks later. Devastated, desperate, and at the bottom of the pit emotionally and mentally, he sought help through ministry. The Holy Spirit helped him forgive himself, his parents, and his ex-wives. The power of the inherited iniquities was broken and the vows reversed. Jesus addressed his trauma memories and reassured Matt that he had believed a lie that he was alone. The truth was he was never alone and he was deeply loved. Matt believed Jesus, embraced this truth, and let it sink deep into his spirit. He said, "I have got to go to every dark corner where Jesus is shining the light, clean the closet, and pull out the skeletons. I have people to make it right with and I want to be a good dad and husband." With God's help he made right the wrong he had done and, not long afterwards, remarried Jane. He has permanent peace and joy!

There are many Christians out there who have been wounded deeply. Most of them believe they will have to live with those wounds forever. Now you know you don't have to. There is freedom in Jesus Christ, not just for salvation, but also from the wounds of this life. Jesus wants to free you. He alone can deliver you.

Think about it:

1. Everyone has a place or places that need healing. Most can name them readily, but some traumas are buried deeply.

2. Ask the Holy Spirit to bring to your mind traumas that have affected your life.

3. Make a brief list of these to share with a trusted, experienced ministry partner. These traumas that have wounded and scarred can be healed.

CHAPTER TWELVE

DELIVERANCE AND PRAYERS

W e try never to evangelize for deliverance. We feel that a person must come to the realization of the need for deliverance through conviction in their own spirit and soul by the leading of the Holy Spirit. In our seminars and classes, we let people know that deliverance is available and as they learn much of what you have been reading, they understand the freedom that comes with deliverance. Most people are aware of the torment and oppression they have been dealing with in their lives for many years.

Through our classes and seminars they become aware that there is a remedy for their pain. That remedy is the freedom only Jesus can give. Most people don't seek freedom until they're at the bottom of the pit. They usually are so far down, there's no way to go but up. They just want peace. They have been in bondage to sin for so long and in misery and torment so deeply that they know they cannot get themselves out. And that is just the place where God can show His power and receive all the glory. He wants them to understand that

He is the only One Who can set them free and give them permanent peace!

We'd like to give a glimpse into the process that is used in this ministry. Other deliverance ministries may differ slightly in their steps to freedom. This may assist the reader to understand where specific aspects of the deliverance process take place.

We make sure the one seeking deliverance understands that we are not the deliverer. We are instruments. The Lord Jesus Christ is the Deliverer. As the Holy Spirit leads, we teach, ask questions, comment, and pray, but the Lord Jesus Christ is the Deliverer and we are all entirely dependent on Him. Jesus Christ has all authority in heaven and on earth. The Holy Spirit has the power to do what needs to be done to the one seeking deliverance and to the enemy.

We then pray that the Holy Spirit will bring to their minds all the things they need to be aware of as we enter into this time together. We pray for protection and for no interference from the enemy during the ministry session.

Then, one by one we take each open door and seek the help of the Lord to close it. Usually, we take the open doors in this order: Willful Disobedience, Inherited Iniquities, Inner Vows and Judgments, Careless Invasion of Enemy Territory, and then Unforgiveness and Trauma. There is a reason for the order.

When anyone is willfully disobedient, they are in rebellion against God. The Holy Spirit brings each act of willful disobedience to their minds. They then acknowledge their sin, confess it, repent of it, and seek forgiveness from God before they can ask Him to do anything about the other open doors.

The soul is made up of the mind, will, and emotions. Those who have unhealthy soul-ties are soul-tied or bonded to people who dominate them or with whom they have an unnatural or super-intense friendship or dependency relationship. Fornication and other sexual sins always form unhealthy soul-ties. A dominating relationship with a parent or spouse can also produce a soul-tie. It is putting us under the influence or control of someone other than God.

Inherited iniquities deal with the tendency and propensity for sin which has been passed down through our forefathers. The one seeking deliverance acknowledges this and asks for forgiveness and release from these inherited iniquities.

The Holy Spirit then brings to mind all inner vows the person has made along with the judgments that accompanied them. Inner vows and judgments are confessed, repented of, and broken. The one seeking deliverance asks the Lord for forgiveness for the vows and judgments that were made, and the Holy Spirit breaks the effect of the inner vows and judgments in their life.

Careless invasion of enemy territory is confessed, repented of, and the Lord is asked for forgiveness.

Unforgiveness and trauma usually go together. If a person has unforgiveness toward someone, most often they associate that person with a trauma of some kind: abuse, rape, betrayal, etc. If there has been trauma in a person's life, many times they have unforgiveness toward the one who was involved. First, a list is made of each person that needs to be forgiven. As the person to be forgiven comes up, usually the trauma also comes up. The trauma is then dealt with. This is where Jesus is invited into the memory and asked to shine His light of truth on the lies associated with the trauma.

Forgiveness invites Jesus to heal the person from the bitterness of unforgiveness and the truth of Jesus heals the pain from the trauma.

At this point, the open doors have been closed and the enemy is profoundly weakened because they have no more right or legal ground to stay. Specific evil spirits have been identified throughout this process. These are then commanded to leave in the name of Jesus Christ and by the power of the Holy Spirit. They must go. They have no legal right to stay. The Lord Jesus Christ has delivered, healed, and given freedom!

If you are seeking to be delivered, remember that it is always best to go through deliverance with an experienced, mature Christian. If you are considering helping others to be delivered, you must first be set free yourself. Free people free people. Deliverance is usually better done by a team of two or more. To guard against emotional attachments, we believe men should minister to men and women should minister to women.

In this section, we are including prayers for the closing of each door. We will provide specific prayers for different situations and attacks of the enemy. Earlier in our lives, we came from a background that was anti-liturgical. That meant any prayers or creeds that were written by someone else were not to be used in our worship or privately. We now, however, find books of prayers and some creedal statements to be very helpful and refreshing. Taking the position that we cannot read someone else's prayer is like saying we cannot sing someone else's songs, and we do that all the time privately and in worship assemblies. These prayers capture the thoughts that our hearts long to express. When we use prayers that were written by someone else, we need to take the time to read over them first and understand what we will be reading and expressing. Then, from the heart, we read through the prayer agreeing with the thoughts and attitudes and offering it up to God through the Lord Jesus Christ.

Most of these prayers are based entirely on God's Word. There is great power in the praying of God's Word aloud. His Word is heard in the spirit realm and it gives life! The enemy shudders when he hears God's Word. He understands the authority, power, and life it brings. The enemy doesn't want us to realize the power God's Word brings to us because we then become dangerous adversaries to his objectives to kill, steal, destroy, confuse our minds, and counterfeit the truth.

Prayer to break an ungodly vow:

Father, I have sinned in ignorance by making a vow. I have passed judgment on (person's name) and I know that is not pleasing to You. My heart was hard and stubborn. I was afraid, angry, and hurt and decided in my own strength to make sure that I was not hurt again. I have unknowingly given room for the enemy to use this vow to hurt me and my relationships with others and with You. I set up a false protection and trusted in myself instead of trusting You. You are the only One that is in control. I ask You to forgive me. I ask You to cancel the vow of (name the vow) in the name of Jesus Christ. Please cancel any rights or authority that I have given the enemy to gain control. Thank You for forgiving me because of the blood of Jesus Christ. With Your help and in Your power, I ask for the grace not to repeat this or behave the way (person's name) did who wounded me. I forgive (person's name) because You have forgiven me. I ask You to bless (person's name). I thank You and praise You for restoring my relationship with You. In the name of Jesus Christ I thank You. Amen

Prayer against receiving negative words of death and lies instead of life:

Father, I have disobeyed You in ignorance by receiving and believing negative words spoken to me by others or from me toward myself. I have allowed the enemy to use them to build a stronghold in my life. I turn away and cancel these words: (name the words). In the name of Jesus Christ, I break the power of these words that the enemy has used to hurt me. I thank You, Father, for restoring my mind because I am who You say that I am. Thank you for speaking life into me. I pray this in the precious name of Jesus Christ. Amen.

Prayer to break unhealthy soul ties:

The soul is made up of the mind, will, and emotions. Those who are soul-tied are bonded to people who dominate them, or with whom they have an unnatural or super-intense friendship or dependency relationship. It is putting yourself under the influence or control of someone other than God. Heavenly Father, I confess the sin of (unhealthy involvement, fornication, or codependent relationship) with (person's first and last name). Through the power of the Holy Spirit, please separate my soul, body, and spirit from the soul, body, and spirit of (person's full name). Please forgive me and remove the ground I have given to the enemy through this wrong relationship. Please bless me and (person's full name) with fulfilling our lives in and through You alone. In the name of Jesus Christ I pray. Amen.

Prayer for confession and repentance of disobedience:

Dear Father, I agree with You that I made a decision with my free will to turn against and ignore You and Your words of truth. Today, I choose to agree with You and Your words of truth. You have said that no sin will have power over me. I turn away from the sin of (name the sin). Please forgive me and cleanse me by the blood of Jesus Christ. By Your grace, I am dead to this sin. I receive the power of the cross through which I am crucified to the world. With Your help and Your power I will walk in Your freedom and receive Your forgiveness. Thank You Lord! Amen.

Prayer for sexual sins:

Lord Jesus Christ, I repent for using my body, which is Your temple for Your Holy Spirit, for ungodly purposes and as an avenue for lust. I choose now to give You my eyes, mouth, mind, heart, hands, feet, and sexual organs as instruments of righteousness. I present to You my whole body as a living sacrifice, holy and acceptable, and I choose to save the sexual use of my body for marriage only (Heb. 13:4). I recognize the lie from the enemy that my body is not clean or holy or acceptable to You because of my past sexual sins. Lord, thank You that You have forgiven and totally cleansed me. Thank You for loving me and accepting me just as I am. Help me to accept myself and my body as cleansed in Your eyes. In the powerful name of Jesus Christ I pray. Amen.

Prayer to break inherited iniquities:

Father, as Your child I cancel out all the demonic working that has been passed down to me and my family. The specific areas of iniquities are: (list the areas of sin and iniquities the Lord has shown you). By the authority I have in Jesus Christ, I now command every spirit assigned to me and my family to leave my presence and go where Jesus Christ sends them. Lord, You said I have been crucified with Jesus Christ and I sit with Him in heavenly places, so I renounce and cancel all assignments from the enemy that have been directed to me and my family in the name of Jesus Christ and with the power of the Holy Spirit. Christ became a curse for me when He died because of my sins on the cross. I belong to the Lord Jesus Christ Who purchased me with His own blood. I declare that I am fully signed over and committed to the Lord forever. I commit myself, with the power of the Holy Spirit, to be obedient and to trust You. In Jesus Christ's name I pray. Amen.

Prayers for forgiving others:

Father, (person's name) has hurt me in this way: (list the words and actions). I choose now to release (person's name) into Your hands. Your ways are perfect in justice and mercy and mine are not. I forgive from my mind, will, and emotions and deep in my heart (person's name) for all of these things he/she has done because You have already forgiven me for what I have done. You said in Your Word (Eph. 6:12) that the battle is not against people. It is with the enemy. Please forgive me for my pride and fear and for taking Your place in judgment. This is Your business. You are in control. I am willing to pay for the emotional pain that this has caused. I ask You, Lord Jesus Christ, to take back the ground I have given to the enemy by believing the lies and allowing this to become a stronghold. Please forgive me for grieving Your Spirit. Please bless (person's name) with the fruits of Your Spirit, Your wisdom, and Your discernment. Thank You for the peace You are giving me as I obey You and give You back Your rightful place in my heart. It is in the precious name of Jesus Christ I pray. Amen.

Prayers for forgiving myself:

Father in heaven, I have done (list the things you have done to yourself and the lies you believed). I agree with You that this was wrong. With Your help, I forgive myself from deep in my heart and let myself go free. I release myself to You. Your mercy is far greater than mine. Because I believed the lies of the enemy, I have allowed the accuser to torment me about this. You have said You love me with a love I can't even grasp. Help me to truly believe this, not just in my head but with all my heart. Thank You that You have already forgiven me through Jesus Christ. Amen.

Prayer about blaming God:

I confess that I have blamed You and held bitterness toward You, God, for allowing things in my life that have been painful and seemed overwhelming to me. Thank You that You have already forgiven me for my bitterness toward you. I accept Your forgiveness and Your patience toward me. I release You, God, from blame for the things that have happened in my life. Help me praise You and believe Your promises that You will work all things for good because I love You and I am Your child. In the name of Jesus Christ I pray. Amen.

Warfare Armor prayer:

Heavenly Father, Your warrior prepares for battle. Today I claim victory over Satan by putting on the whole armor of God! I put on truth that I may stand firm in the truth of Your Word so I will not be a victim of Satan's lies. I put on righteousness to guard my heart from evil so I will remain pure and holy, protected under the blood of Jesus Christ. I put on peace that I may stand firm in the good news of the Gospel so Your peace will shine through me and be a light to all I encounter. I put on faith in order to be ready for Satan's fiery darts of doubt, denial, and deceit so I will not be vulnerable to spiritual defeat. I put on salvation so I can keep my mind focused on You and the enemy will not have a stronghold on my thoughts. I take the two-edged sword of the Spirit, Your Word, to be ready in my hands to expose the tempting words of Satan. Thank you for Your protection so I can live in spiritual victory! In the powerful name of Jesus Christ. Amen. (Author unknown.)

EPILOGUE

You are a child of the Living God. You have been given authority to live and act in the name of the Lord Jesus Christ. You are indwelt by the power of the Holy Spirit. When the doors are closed and the spirits are cast out, there is peace and freedom. The abundant life you've always wanted but never dreamed possible will be yours in Christ. Don't wait in misery and torment. The oppression and harassment of the enemy will stop, but you've got to let Jesus free you. He is the great Deliverer. He wants to free you now.

God bless you on your journey to peace and freedom. The Lord Jesus Christ has given you salvation and victory over the grave. Let Him give you freedom and abundant life. Let Him break the bonds that enslave you.

BIBLIOGRAPHY

Neil T. Anderson, The Bondage Breaker (Eugene, OR: Harvest House Publishers, 2000).

Dr. Henry Malone, Shadow Boxing (Irving, TX: Vision Life Publications, 1999).

Dr. Henry Malone, Freedom and Fullness Seminar (Irving, TX: Vision Life Ministries, 1995).

John Regier, Biblical Concepts Counseling Workbook -- Identifying and Resolving Personal and Marital Problems Biblically (Colorado Springs, CO: www.biblicalconcepts.org, 1999).

Lester Sumrall, Demons - the Answer Book (New Kensington, PA: Lester Sumrall Evangelistic Association, Inc., 1993).

Charles Kraft, I Give You Authority -- Practicing the Authority Jesus Gave Us (Grand Rapids, MI: Chosen Books, a Division of Baker Book House Co., 1997).

John Eldredge, Waking the Dead (Nashville, TN: Thomas Nelson, Inc., 2003).

Everett Cox, Spiritual Warfare Attack Team (Oklahoma City, OK: Deliverance Ministries, Inc., 2004).

**For Speaking Engagements
please call (334) 398-0268**

BOOK ORDER FORM

Send to:

PAUL AND CAROLYN BLOUNT
RELEASED
5345 Atlanta Hwy
Montgomery, AL 36109-3323

JOHN 3:36

Please send me _____ copies of **Released: Finding Freedom and Peace Through Jesus Christ** by Paul and Carolyn Blount, at the rate of $15.00 each, plus shipping charges noted below.

Name_____

Address_____

_____

City _____

State _____ Zip _____

SHIPPING CHARGES

Quantity of Books	Shipping Charge
1	$3.00
2-3	$4.00
4-6	$6.00
7-9	$7.00
10-25	FREE